I0569269

My Journey Beyond the Well

Grace • Identity • Purpose

by
Pamela Bowen

Acknowledgments

There are some journeys you don't walk alone—
and this one?
It was carried by the prayers, love, and strength of so
many.

To my Family
You are the heartbeat of this story.

To my Husband, Kevin
My rock. My greatest supporter.
Your transformation has been one of the most powerful
redemptions I've ever witnessed.
You are proof that God doesn't just restore—He exceeds
every expectation.

To my Children
Your strength and resilience inspire me daily.
Watching God move in your lives has been my greatest
joy.
You are living testimonies that healing, hope, and purpose
are possible.

To my Parents
Momma, thank you for showing me how to survive and
thrive through every storm life may throw my way—and
for being present through them all.

Daddy, thank you for the magic of my early years when I
was your #1.
Those memories helped shape the light in me that still
shines today.

To my longtime Pastors, Ron and Hope Carpenter
Your leadership reaches into broken places and speaks life.
Your influence has enriched every part of my life and the lives of my family.
Thank you for leading with authenticity, wisdom, and healing power.

To the Inner Circle Ladies
Thank you for your encouragement when my faith felt tested.
Your sisterhood has been a covering of strength, prayer, and divine support.

To my Sister in Christ, Kathy
Thank you for always encouraging me to pursue God's calling on my life.

To Pastor Kimberly Jones (Real Talk Kim)
Your morning prayer sessions lit a fire in me to rise, write, and pour out for the Kingdom.

This book would not be what it is without the power of those mornings.

And to you, Dear Reader
This book is for you.

For every woman who has ever felt forgotten.
For every heart that's ever sat alone at the well,
wondering if redemption is still possible.
For every soul longing to know:
Does my story still matter?

Yes. It does.

May these words remind you that grace still finds us in
the wilderness.

That your voice still matters.
And that the One who met her at the well
still waits to meet you, too.

And finally—

To the One who met me at the well and never left...
Every word I've written belongs to You.
I am forever grateful.

—**Pamela Bowen**

Interior formatting by Kevin Bowen
Cover design and concept by Pamela Bowen

Unless otherwise indicated, all Scripture references are taken from the King James Version (KJV) of the Holy Bible and are used by permission.

This book is a work of personal testimony, reflection, and biblical insight. While inspired by true events, names and identifying details may have been changed to protect the privacy of individuals.

The opinions expressed are those of the author.

Printed in the United States of America
First Edition: 2025
ISBN: 978-1-968912-02-4

For more resources, speaking inquiries, or to connect with the author, email: pamelabowenauthor@gmail.com

Introduction: Come Meet Him at the Well

Some of the most life-changing conversations happen when we least expect them—in places we'd rather avoid, carrying jars we were never meant to hold.

"he must needs go through Samaria" – John 4:4 (KJV)

There are moments in life when everything changes—not because of what we've done, but because of who we encounter.

This book was born from one of those moments.

Like the Samaritan woman, I didn't go looking for a Savior that day. I was just trying to survive—one more day, one more decision, one more trip to the well. But Jesus met me in the middle of my mess.

He didn't wait for me to get it all together. He didn't demand perfection. He simply sat down beside me and started a conversation that would change my life.

You'll find my story on these pages. It's messy. It's honest.

And it's full of the kind of redemption that only God can write. But this book isn't just about me—and it's not just about her, the woman at the well.

It's about *you.*

It's about the jars you've carried.
The shame you've buried.

The questions you've been too afraid to ask.
The dreams you're scared to hope for.
The parts of you that feel invisible or unworthy.

If you've ever wondered whether Jesus would meet
someone like *you* at the well—this book is your answer.

He will.
He does.
And He's waiting right now.

This book is divided into three parts:

- Part One: What We Carry to the Well – explores the burdens, shame, and hidden wounds we bring with us.

- Part Two: When He Meets Us There – reveals how Jesus enters our brokenness, confronts our pain, and begins the healing.

- Part Three: What We Leave Behind and Walk Into – invites you to lay it all down and step boldly into your identity, your calling, and your freedom.

In each chapter, you'll find scripture reflections, journaling prompts, prayers, and questions designed to help you pause, breathe, and connect deeply with Jesus in your own journey.

You don't need to *rush*.
You don't need to *perform*.
You're not too far gone.
You're not too late.
You're not too broken.
You're invited.

Come meet Him at the well.

Let Him tell you who you really are.

Let Him show you what grace can do with your story.

Let this book be more than a message—let it become a moment of encounter.

You're not just holding pages.

You're holding an invitation.

Part One
The Search for Worth

Before the Story Unfolds...
This is where everything truly begins—Not at the moment of breakthrough, not at the altar of healing, but in the hollow spaces of longing.

It begins in the silence that follows rejection.
In the restless wondering if you'll ever be enough.
In the moments when love felt like something you had to chase, and worth felt just out of reach.

Before grace ever found your name, before purpose ever took shape—There was the ache.
And it's here, in the ache, that the story starts.

These next few chapters walk through the places I once tried to forget— The shadows I carried, the silence I lived in, and the way I shaped myself around people who never truly saw me.

Maybe you've done that too.
Maybe you've tried to hold your breath in relationships—shrinking yourself just to be chosen.

Maybe you've told yourself, If I can just hold it all together, maybe I'll be enough.

I know that lie. I lived it.

But this is the beginning of the unraveling, the peeling back, the slow and sacred revealing of the places we carry pain and call it normal.

You don't have to hide here.
This is where we meet the woman at the well—still carrying shame, still thirsty, still hoping someone might stay.

And this is where we begin to believe... Maybe **Jesus isn't going anywhere.**

So take a deep breath.
This isn't just *my story.*
It's *ours now.*

Let's begin.

Chapter 1
When Shame Speaks First

The Silent Weight of Rejection

I can't point to the exact moment I first felt unwanted, because it wasn't just one moment.
It was a quiet ache that followed me like a shadow, slipping into memories where love should've lived.
Not loud... but constant.
A presence that whispered, "You don't belong," long before I ever understood what belonging meant.

It's a strange thing to carry rejection so young.
It settles into your bones before you even know how to name it.
Before you can understand what it means, you already believe it must be your fault—that something about you is just too much... or not enough.

I didn't grow up with the kind of rejection you can brush off. It wasn't a playground insult or the sting of being picked last in gym class. It was deeper, more personal, more defining.
It was the kind of rejection that doesn't just bruise your heart—it reshapes your sense of self.

Home felt fragile.
Like something I had to tiptoe through.

I became an expert at reading the atmosphere—sensing
the storm before it even reached the room.
I knew the tone in my mother's voice that meant the walls
were closing in.

I knew how to disappear when the tension got too thick.

Even as a little girl, I was already learning the art of
disappearing.
Not in body—but in spirit.
I learned how to quiet my needs.
How to soften my presence.

When Love Feels Conditional

Love, to me, felt like something I had to earn—through
perfection. Through performance.
Through becoming exactly what someone else needed me
to be.

I believed love was fragile, easily broken, that once it
slipped through your fingers, you could never get it back.

The Generational Weight

My mother loved me—I know that.
But her love came through the *filter of her own wounds.*
And wounded love... bleeds.

She knew rejection intimately.
Abandoned by her father.
Left to wonder if anyone would ever truly stay.
She was married at fifteen—still a child herself.
And by nineteen, her first two babies had been taken from
her, raised by their grandparents.

By the time I was born, my mother was already drowning
in rejection, in disappointment, in heartbreak that hadn't
healed.
And when you're drowning... you can't hold anyone else
above water.

Her brokenness became the lens through which she loved
me. And though I was too young to understand the
weight of her story—I could feel it pressing down on me.

Clinging to Love

She clung to me—not out of nurturing, but out of desperation.
I was her second chance.
Her proof that maybe love could stay this time.
Her lifeline...
Her hope that someone wouldn't leave.

But children aren't meant to save their parents.
And when love comes with that kind of weight—it stops feeling like love. And starts feeling like survival.

Well Reflection – The Weight of What we Carry

- Who carried you while you were carrying the weight of others?

- When did you first realize you had been trying to earn love?

- What parts of your story still feel heavy with the responsibility you were never meant to carry?

What Children Carry

When parents are drowning, their children become the life raft. And they carry the weight of saving someone they were never meant to save.

I became a fixer before I even knew what that meant.
I learned how to sense her moods before she spoke.
I learned how to shrink my needs, swallow my emotions, and become whatever I needed to be.

God's Provision in My Grandparents

But God—Oh, how I **love** those two words.
Because even in the chaos, ***God provided a refuge.***
My grandparents became my safe place.

Their home was steady when everything else was crumbling.
They didn't need me to fix them.
They didn't ask me to shrink.
They just loved me—with a love that didn't require performance in return.

Saturday Mornings and Safe Love

Every weekend, my Father would pick me up from my
Mom's and take me to my Grandparents' house—where he
lived. Saturday mornings became sacred.
I would wake to the smell of coffee brewing and the
sound of cartoons drifting from the living room.
My Grandfather would be in the kitchen whistling some
old tune, while making "eggs in a basket," His specialty.

He gave me silly nicknames, and told corny jokes that
didn't make sense... And I laughed like they were the
funniest things in the world.
His love was simple, steady, safe...
And safe love says you don't have to earn this.
You are wanted here. You belong.

Bedtime Stories and Imagination

At night, my Grandmother would tuck me in.
Her small frame perched gently on the edge of my bed,
telling stories from a childhood shaped by the Great
Depression.

Her stories were wild, magical, larger than life.
They weren't just bedtime stories—they were lifelines.
They taught me that imagination could build a door
when life only gave you walls.
Storytelling heals when life feels unbearable.
Stories become a way to breathe hope into the darkness.

Loss and the Lingering Ache

When they died—first my Grandfather from cancer when
I was in my twenties, then my Grandmother followed him
years later—it felt like the earth shifted beneath my feet.

Their love had been my anchor. My proof that
unconditional love was real. That it could last.
Without them I felt untethered—adrift in a world that felt
harsh, unsteady, and so unkind.

Even now, I sometimes close my eyes and find myself
back in their kitchen—swinging my legs at the counter,
watching my grandfather cook eggs in a basket.

That's the thing about safe love—it leaves fingerprints on
your soul that time can't erase.
But even with all the love they gave me, there were
wounds no human could heal.
There were cracks so deep... they needed Living Water to
fill them.

As much as I tried to live off their love,
It couldn't undo the deeper story of rejection
that had already taken root inside me.
And that story?
It would follow me—into every relationship, every
attempt to find security, every desperate search for
someone to finally choose me... and never let me go.

- Who were the people God placed in your life as safe places?

- What did their love teach you about real belonging?

- Did it reveal a kind of grace you never thought you'd experience?

"For I will pour water upon him that is thirsty, and floods upon the dry ground..." — Isaiah 44:3 (KJV)

A Stepmother's Cruelty and a Father's Betrayal

There was a time when my father was my safe place.
My weekend hero.

The man who called me his "number one." I would look forward to him picking me up on Fridays.

It felt like a break from reality—a pocket of normal in a world that rarely felt stable. When he picked me up from my mom's house he took me somewhere safe—somewhere full of love.

But even my safe place wouldn't stay safe for long.

A New Chapter That Changed Everything

She was his girlfriend—living with her grandparents.
He was older, already in his thirties, still trying to find his
way while living at my grandparents' house.

Somewhere along the way, she got pregnant.
And my little sister was born.
I was excited. The idea of having a sister felt like a gift.
I imagined weekends full of giggles and shared secrets.
Something special we could have together.

But when her grandparents passed away, everything
changed.

*She had nowhere to go—so my father moved her and my
sister into an apartment.*

That's when the dynamic shifted.
I was no longer the center of his world.
His attention changed. His energy shifted.
And slowly, I began to feel it—the ache of being replaced.
The quiet message: You're no longer the priority.

I still visited. But I never truly felt welcome in their new
life. So I stayed where I was always wanted—at my
grandparents' house.

And every time I stepped into their apartment, the
tension met me at the door.
Unspoken, heavy, and always present.

Her rejection wasn't subtle.
It was loud—without a single word.
I don't want you here.

The Wedding Album I Was Never Meant to See

Years later, the truth hit harder than I could've imagined.
It was just another weekend visit.
I was getting ready to go skating—big hair, hairspray. You
know, the 80s in full swing.

I opened the cabinet under the bathroom sink to grab the
Aqua Net—but instead... I found a photo album.

It was tucked in the back like a secret.
I opened it. And page after page.
Wedding photos, smiles, rings, celebration.
But no me.
No invitation, no explanation.
No one told me they had gotten married.
No one thought I mattered enough to include.
Or even to tell.

When Secrets Speak Louder Than Words

Sometimes the hardest part of rejection isn't what's said—it's what's hidden.

The silence that tells you exactly where you stand.

When I confronted my father with the album in hand, he looked me in the eyes and lied.
"It's not real."
"It was just for fun."
"They were playing dress-up."

But I knew.
And that day... something inside me cracked.
I didn't scream. I didn't cry.
I just... withdrew.

I stopped asking for space in his life.
And I stayed with the ones who always made room for me—my grandparents.

Where I had a room of my own.
My own place. My own sense of worth.

Over time, her hostility hardened.
She didn't just dislike me—She wanted me gone.

And my father?
He chose silence.
He chose peace in his home

Over protection for his daughter.
But there's a price to pay when peace is kept at the expense of the innocent.

"But whoso shall offend one of these little ones which believe in me, it were better for him that a millstone were hanged about his neck, and that he were drowned in the depth of the sea."

— Matthew 18:6 (KJV)

The Legacy of Rejection

Years later when I was in my 40's she passed away, and her jealousy still tried to speak through her children.

Her youngest daughter called my son with a message for me, "Tell your mother she better not show up at my mom's funeral."

Even in death... Rejection had found a voice.
It had become her legacy—passed down like a bitter inheritance no child ever deserves.
And in that moment, I felt it all over again.
That ache I had known since I was a child—the ache of being unwelcome. The ache of not belonging.

Even as a grown woman...
They still wanted me to feel like I didn't belong.

Jesus Understands Rejection

Rejection doesn't just hurt—it becomes a filter.
It shapes how you see yourself, how you expect others to treat you, and what you believe you deserve.

It teaches you to expect abandonment.
To assume love will always walk away.
But I've learned something sacred on this healing journey:
Jesus understands rejection.

He came to His own—the very people He created, the ones He loved, the ones He came to save—and they cast Him aside.

"He came unto His own, and His own received Him not." –
John 1:11 (KJV)

He was rejected, abandoned, misunderstood—even by those closest to Him.

Jesus Knows

There is **no rejection** *you've endured that Jesus Himself hasn't walked through.*

When my father turned away from me, **Jesus stayed.**

When my stepmother tried to erase me, **Jesus wrote my name on His hand.**
When rejection tried to define my story, Jesus became my rescue.

Well Reflection – When Rejection Tries to Rewrite Your Worth

- When did you first feel replaced or pushed aside by someone you loved?

- Have you ever felt silenced by someone choosing peace over protection?

- What room—real or symbolic—did God give you to call your own?

These aren't just questions—they're *keys.*

Let them unlock the spaces within you still carrying the ache of being overlooked.

Then listen closely… because **God has always had a place with your name on it.**

"In my Father's house are many rooms… I go to prepare a place for you." — John 14:2 (KJV)

The Woman at the Well—A Mirror of My Own Pain

She came at noon—not because she preferred the heat,
but because no one else would be there.
She carried more than a water jar.
She carried shame, stares, and a reputation that walked
into town before she did.

She was the woman they warned their daughters about.

The one who couldn't keep a man.
The one with a past. The one no one wanted to sit beside.

And maybe... She believed every word they said.
Because **when rejection becomes your identity, shame
becomes your shadow.**

I know that shadow.
I carried it too.
Every time my stepmother's glare pierced through me.
Every time my father chose silence over protection.

*Like her, I knew what it felt like to be the outsider, the
inconvenience.*

She didn't expect anyone to be at the well that day.
She especially *didn't expect Him.*
A Jewish man—sitting right there at her well.

A man who, by every cultural rule, should have ignored
her, looked away, pretended she didn't exist.

But this man didn't look away. He looked into her.

Like He was seeing everything—every man, every mistake, every label, and every tear.
And somehow...He didn't flinch.

A Word for the One Who Feels Unwanted

Dear Reader,

I see you—the one who's been carrying the weight of rejection like it's your name.
Why silence feels louder than words.
But I need you to know something sacred: Jesus sees you.
Right here. Right now.
He sees the way *you've hidden your pain.*
The walls you've built to keep the hurt out.
And He's *not looking away.*

He's sitting at your well—not to condemn you, but to redeem you. Not to reject you, but to redefine you.

Come unto me, all ye that labour and are heavy laden, and I will give you rest. Matthew 11:28 (KJV)

Jesus wants you to know:

You are seen.
You are wanted.

You are chosen.
You are beloved.

Lay down the lie that you are unworthy.

Let Him rewrite every label.

Let Him speak truth into every wounded place.

Let Him show you... You were never invisible to Him.
Not for one moment.

Facing the Ache – When Rejection First Entered

Rejection doesn't always slam the door.
Sometimes, it leaves it cracked—just wide enough to
wonder why no one came looking for you.

You learned early how to adjust yourself to stay wanted.
How to read moods like maps, how to disappear without
leaving the room.

Love became something you auditioned for.
A prize for the perfect version of you.
And every time it slipped through your fingers, you didn't
just question love—you questioned yourself.

You didn't ask for the ache.
It was handed to you..

Passed down through generations like an unspoken heirloom.
And somewhere between childhood and womanhood, you started answering to names that were never yours: Unwanted, inconvenient, too much, not enough.

But here's what's true:
You were not invisible.
Not to God.
Not for a single moment.

Every time you were overlooked, He leaned in closer.
Every time someone withheld love, He poured out more.

And even when you couldn't feel Him—He was there.

 "When my father and my mother forsake me, then the Lord will take me up." — Psalm 27:10 (KJV)

Pour It Out – Letting Jesus Rewrite the Story

Take a quiet moment and reflect.
Write a letter to the one who made you feel unwanted.
Be honest. Say what you've never said out loud.

Then—release them into God's hands.
Let Jesus rewrite the story rejection tried to define.

Then... write a letter from Jesus to you.
Let His words speak directly to your worth, Your identity, and the truth the enemy tried to silence.
Let Him remind you of who you are, whose you are, and how deeply you are loved.

A Prayer for the One Who Feels Unseen

Lord,
You see the one reading these words—the one who's been told, directly or silently, that they were not wanted.
.

The one who became a fixer, a pleaser, carrying the weight of others' wounds before understanding her own.

You saw her at the well long before she ever knew Your name.

So today, would You **wrap her in truth?**

Not just gentle words, but **deep healing truth**.

Remind her that she was never meant to disappear.

That her voice matters.
That her story matters.
That her presence carries weight in the Kingdom of Heaven.

For every place where rejection tried to write her
identity—whisper louder still:
You are chosen.
You are cherished.
You are mine.
Help her lay down the labels.
Undo the lies.
And restore the wonder of who she really is in You.
Let the ache she carries become a well of Living Water—
where shame is rinsed away, and belovedness flows
freely.

Hold her close, Jesus.
And never let her forget:
She was never unwanted.
She was always Yours.
Amen.

The Search for Stability

I was fifteen when I got married.
Young, naive, wounded from rejection and searching for
something—anything—that looked like love.

Then I met him, he was eighteen, charismatic, handsome.
The kind of guy who could talk his way into or out of
anything.

He had a way of making me feel like I was the only one in
the world. And when you've grown up feeling like a
burden, being someone's everything feels like a miracle.

He said he would give me a better life.
And I believed him.
Because I needed to.

What I didn't know was that he was broken, too.
The only child of divorced parents, raised in dysfunction,
carrying his own invisible wounds.

He didn't wear those wounds on his sleeve—not at first.
At first, he wore charm, confidence, and possibility.

But promises fade fast when pain is driving the person making them. And not long into our marriage, that better life turned into a nightmare.

The Beginning of the Abuse

He became addicted to crack cocaine.
And with the drugs came paranoia, rage, and violence.
He locked me in the house. He controlled who I saw, where I went, and how I existed.

He beat me, screamed at me, broke things, and piece by piece, he broke me too.

What started as a promise turned into a prison.
And I was trapped. Pregnant, terrified, and all alone.

The Death of My First Child

In the middle of that chaos, I gave birth to my first child.

A beautiful baby girl. She was the one thing that gave me hope. The one reason I still believed something good could come from my pain.
And for a few precious months—she was my joy, my anchor, my reminder that love could exist in the middle of heartbreak.

But then, suddenly she was gone.
Sudden Infant Death Syndrome.

Three words that sound clinical.

But they shattered my entire world.
One day, she was breathing.
The next, I was holding her lifeless body in my arms,
Screaming into a silence that would echo for years.
I had already lost myself.
Now I had lost my daughter, too.

The Spiral That Followed

Her death didn't change him. It made him worse.
He spiraled deeper into his addiction. The abuse
intensified. And I became invisible in my own grief.

Then came another pregnancy. Another loss.
A miscarriage that left me physically bleeding
and emotionally numb. I was still just a child myself— But
somehow I knew... if I didn't leave, I wasn't going to
survive.

Well Reflection – When Pain Outstays Its Welcome

- Have you ever stayed in something damaging
  because it once felt like love?

- What parts of you had to "break free" before you
  physically could?

- What moment gave you the courage to believe
  there had to be more?

28

I gathered what little courage I had left when I got pregnant with my third child—and I ran.

I found a women's shelter, left the state, and started over while pregnant again—carrying a child I was determined to protect.

Carrying a heart that still beat with grief, but also with something fragile and brave: Hope.

A New Relationship, A New Pain

By the time I met my second husband, I was 21 years old. My daughter—my miracle after so much loss—was about a year old. I was rebuilding my life—slowly, imperfectly, but with intention.

I met him through his sister who was married to his best friend. Both of them were in the Navy at the time we met. He was handsome, the soft-spoken type.
And after surviving years of chaos, Just being around someone who didn't rage or belittle me felt like peace

He had grown up around church, but his story with church was complicated. As a teenager, he had looked up to a pastor who later fell into sexual sin.

That failure left a scar—the kind that makes you question what's real and what's just performance.

But when we got serious, he wanted to do things the right way.

And I saw that as a sign of hope.

We went to a church that followed a denomination he was familiar with—one he hadn't been attending at the time, but it felt like the right place to start fresh.

The church was filled with other Navy families and was located near the base where he was stationed.
It felt like a community that understood us.
Understood the life we were stepping into.

When we got married, our entire wedding party wore Navy uniforms. The wives were my bridesmaids.
The men he served his country with stood proud beside him in dress whites.

It was a beautiful day—and I believed with everything in me that it was the beginning of something new.

When Faith Feels Threatening

What I didn't realize back then was that my relationship with God intimidated him.

He saw how I worshiped, how I trusted God without hesitation, how I poured my heart out in prayer like I was talking to my best friend.

To me, it was just who I was.

To him, it made him feel small.

He began to feel like he couldn't measure up spiritually, emotionally, as a leader, or a husband. And instead of leaning in, he pulled away.

He started chasing validation in places he didn't belong. And eventually, that search led him into betrayal.

The Betrayal I Never Saw Coming

He cheated on me. *Not just with anyone*—with someone I trusted.

Someone who sat beside me *in church.*

Someone who lifted their hands in worship.

Someone who knew my story and still crossed the line.

She was supposed to be a friend.

She was **supposed to be safe.**

And yet, behind my back and under the roof of the spiritual community, the person I had trusted most and the person I had welcomed in wrote another chapter of rejection into my life.

Some of the deepest wounds don't come from the world—
They come from those who know the name of Jesus, but
forget the weight of His love.

- Have you ever trusted again, only to be betrayed
  when you thought you were finally safe?

- Have you ever been wounded by someone in a
  church or spiritual setting?

- How did that experience shape your view of God or
  your trust in the community of faith?

I had already survived abuse, buried a child, escaped addiction and violence. But this?

This betrayal tore something different.
Because this time I had let my guard down.
This time I thought I was doing it right.

This time I thought God had brought me my healing. But instead,

I was left once again with the ache of not being enough.

The ache of being replaced.

The ache of spiritual confusion—wondering how people could raise their hands on Sunday and hold secrets on Monday.

He was young, insecure, unprepared.
But he was not a monster.
He was a good man...who made a deeply wounding choice.

And once again, I was left starting over.

Starting Over Again – Alone but Not Abandoned

I never expected to be here again—alone, bruised, and rebuilding.

But this time, the ache was deeper because I had dared to believe I was safe.

After the betrayal, I found myself alone again

 Another marriage broken.
Another fresh wave of grief.
Another moment of standing in the mirror asking,
 "What's wrong with me?"

I was still so young—
but already so tired of trusting only to be torn again.

But even in that wilderness, God never left me.

I didn't feel strong.
I didn't feel holy.
I didn't feel full of faith.

But I kept showing up—to life, to motherhood, to the next thing in front of me.

And somehow, that was worship too.

Even Silence Is a Sanctuary
Sometimes faith isn't loud.
Sometimes faith is just breathing.
Just choosing not to give up when giving up would be easier.

Well Reflection – The Ache of Being Left Again

- When have you felt like you were doing everything right, only to be hurt anyway?

- What fears rise up when you think about being alone again?

- In what small ways has God continued to show up for you, even in the silence?

There were days I couldn't pray with words—Only tears.

There were nights I lay awake staring at the ceiling,

Asking God to explain why love always seemed to leave me behind.

But I kept going.
Not because I was fearless, but because I couldn't stop believing that maybe, somehow, God still had something for me.

That maybe I wasn't too damaged.
Maybe I wasn't too far gone.
Maybe there was more.
And there was.

It didn't come quickly.
It didn't come easily.
But the God who met a woman at a well in the middle of her shame was the same God who sat beside me In my empty room with a child asleep in the next room, and heartbreak still fresh in my chest.

Jesus didn't just wait for her—He waits for us, too.
At the end of rejection. In the middle of shame.
On the other side of betrayal.

The Woman at the Well – My Story in Hers

I imagine her heart was tired, too.
Five husbands, a live-in partner, a lifetime of whispers
and sideways glances.

She wasn't just known for her past.

She was defined by it. And still, she came to the well.

She didn't know she was walking into redemption.
She didn't know she was about to meet a man who
wouldn't use her, leave her, or define her by her mistakes.
She just came thirsty. Like me.

I had searched for love in all the wrong places.
I had married young, desperate to be seen.
I had been betrayed, lied to, replaced, and discarded.

*And every time I thought I'd found safety, the ground
shifted again.*

But so did she. And yet, Jesus met her anyway.

He didn't look at her the way the others did.
He didn't see her as damaged goods.
He saw her as worthy of a divine encounter.
And what He offered her—Living Water—was the same thing He offered me.
Not just comfort. Not just healing. But identity.

He Didn't Leave Her Empty.
Jesus met her in the middle of her mess, and still gave her the one thing no man ever had: **Value.**

Like the woman at the well, I was exhausted from carrying jar after jar to places that never truly satisfied.

But Jesus saw me, too.
He met me in battered women's shelters, in quiet church pews, and in crowded sanctuaries.

In moments of betrayal, and beginnings of new life.
And when everyone else saw a broken woman—He saw a beloved daughter.

Facing the Ache - When Love and Survival Collide

Some choices aren't made from clarity—they're made from desperation. Not because you didn't know better. But because survival doesn't wait for wisdom.

You didn't walk into those relationships blind.
You walked in bruised.
Hoping this time would be different..

And when it felt like love—for a moment, for a breath—
you clung to it like it was oxygen.
You weren't weak. You were human.

You wanted what every heart longs for: safety, affection, and peace.

 And when it slipped through your fingers again, you didn't just mourn the loss—you mourned the version of you that believed maybe this time... would be enough.

This is the ache of starting over.

Of loving when it costs you more than you knew you had. Of trusting again, only to be handed more pieces than promises.

But hear this:

Your ache is not proof of failure—it's proof that your heart was still open when others had shut down.

It's proof that you haven't given up on love...
Even when love didn't treat you kindly.

God sees it all.
The wounds behind your strength.
The tears behind your silence.
The hope behind your history.
He's not ashamed of the story you carry.

He's already working it into something redemptive—not
in spite of the ache... But through it.

*"He healeth the broken in heart, and bindeth up their
wounds." — Psalm 147:3 (KJV)*

Pour It Out - Exchange Control for Communion

Write a letter to God, surrendering the areas of your life
Where you have sought security outside of Him.
Be honest about your fears, your hurts, and your desires.

Ask Him to fill the empty places with His love and truth.

Then, write a response from Jesus back to you.

What do you imagine He would say to you in love?

A Prayer for the One Who Keeps Starting Over

Lord,
You see the one reading this—the one who has trusted again and again, only to be left holding the pieces.
You know the ache of being betrayed.
You know what it feels like to love someone who doesn't love you well. And You also know what it's like to be misunderstood, abandoned, and alone.

So would You **meet this one—right here in the middle of the heartbreak?**

Wrap them in Your steady, unwavering love.

Show them that they are not too broken to be chosen.

Not too damaged to be desired.

Lift the weight they've been carrying.

Heal the places that still flinch from touch.

And whisper this truth into their soul:

 You are not alone.
 You are not unwanted.
You are not unworthy.

Jesus, be the stability we've been searching for. Amen.

Chapter 3

Face to Face with Grace

After years of chasing love that couldn't last, I began
drawing water from other wells.
Wells of approval, control, distraction, and survival.
But none of them could truly satisfy the ache inside me.

The Moment of Truth

There comes a moment in every story—a moment where
the masks fall off, where the truth is undeniable,
where you can't keep pretending everything's okay.

For me, that moment didn't come all at once.

It came in layers—through tears, through worship,

*Through unexpected encounters with the presence of God
that stripped me bare and didn't shame me for it.*

I had spent years trying to hold it all together.

Trying to prove I was strong.

Trying to outrun the brokenness that clung to me like a
second skin.

But Jesus wasn't asking me to perform.

He wasn't asking for perfection.
He was waiting for honesty.

He was waiting for the real me—the one beneath the survival, beneath the strong front, beneath the guilt, grief, and shame.

And when I finally came undone before Him... He didn't flinch.

He welcomed it.

Well Reflection – The Truth Can Be Terrifying... But It's Also Where Healing Begins

- What's the part of your story you've worked the hardest to hide?

- What would it feel like to let Jesus meet you there—instead of performing for Him?

- What truth have you avoided because you feared rejection, not realizing it's the exact place Jesus wants to heal?

What I Thought God Wanted

I used to believe God wanted perfection, clean hands,
polished prayers, a version of me that didn't cry too
much, or ask too many questions.

I thought He wanted the Sunday version of me—the one
who raised her hands in worship

Even when her heart was breaking in silence.

I believed holiness meant hiding.
That being a "good Christian" meant smiling through pain,
never admitting just how tired I really was.

And I thought if I just tried harder, served more, prayed
more, sacrificed more...

Maybe He would finally bless me.

 Maybe He would finally fix me.

But that wasn't what He wanted at all.

What He Really Wants

God wasn't waiting for me to be polished—He was waiting for me to be honest.

He didn't need the cleaned-up version of me.
He wanted the one still covered in dirt.
Still limping from betrayal.
Still carrying shame I couldn't shake off.

He didn't need a performance. He wanted my surrender.
And when I finally fell apart in front of Him—not just
emotionally, but spiritually—He didn't look away.
He drew closer.

Well Reflection – He Doesn't Need Your Perfection, Just Your Permission

- What have you believed you had to clean up before coming to God?

- In what areas of your life has pressure to stay composed kept you from being real with Him?

- What would it look like to bring your raw, unfiltered heart to Jesus—even in the mess?

That moment with Him wasn't about me getting it together—it was about realizing I never could.

And He loved me anyway.
A Safe Place to Hide

After everything I'd been through—two broken marriages,
betrayal, and the ache of never feeling truly chosen—I
met someone who changed everything.

He was charming, but not in a way that faded or fooled
me. His smile was warm. His presence calming.
He didn't try to impress me—he simply made me feel
seen.

He adored me.
But what stunned me even more... Was how quickly and
completely he adored my daughter too.

This man would become the father of my two youngest
children. And for a season, he became my shelter in a
storm I didn't even know I was still standing in.

He never treated us like baggage.
He treated us like treasure.
And he made sure we felt that every single day.

He wanted a family—this family.
Not an idealized version. Not a fantasy.
He wanted us—the real, scarred, healing, still-standing us.

When I got pregnant, he was thrilled.
He wasn't scared of responsibility.
He leaned into it with joy.

And for the first time in a long time,
I felt chosen—not because I had to earn it.
Not because I had to perform. Just because I was me.

Well Reflection – Real Love Doesn't Need You to Shrink

- What parts of yourself have you felt pressured to hide in order to be loved?

- How did it feel to be accepted—flaws and all?

- Who in your life has reflected God's love by embracing the real you?

But even in the warmth of his acceptance,
Something inside me still felt... empty.

I had spent my life searching for security in relationships, thinking that if I could just find someone who wouldn't break me, I would finally be okay.

That if love didn't come with betrayal, it would be enough to fix what had been shattered inside me.

But was I really healing?
Or was I just finding a softer place to hide?
Because the truth was—even the safest love on earth can't heal a soul wound.

Security says: "You won't be hurt here."

Healing says: "Even if you are, you'll be whole."

Love that isn't rooted in Christ can offer comfort, but only Jesus can make you whole.

- Have you ever mistaken emotional safety for spiritual healing?

- In what ways have you hidden behind "safe" relationships instead of seeking real healing from Jesus?

- What would it look like to let Jesus into the parts of you that even your closest loved ones can't reach?

The God Who Sees Beyond the Surface

The Samaritan woman knew what it was like to be seen by men. But not known. Not loved.
She had spent her life moving from one relationship to another, hoping that maybe the next one would finally be different.

Maybe this time, he won't leave.
Maybe this time, I won't get hurt.
Maybe this time, I'll be enough.
But none of them stayed, none of them satisfied.
And now, she found herself at a well, alone.
Carrying the weight of every heartbreak, every whisper, and every judgment.

"Thou God seest me." – Genesis 16:13 (KJV)

She was used to being overlooked—but Jesus looked directly at her.
She was used to being shamed—but Jesus didn't condemn her.
She was used to hiding—but Jesus called her into the light.

She didn't expect Him.
She didn't expect grace.
She had learned to brace for rejection—to keep her head down and her guard up.

Hadn't every man already proven she was never enough?

Why would this one be any different?

But He was.

He wasn't disgusted by her past.
He wasn't avoiding her like the others did.
He wasn't speaking to her like she was less than.
He looked at her like she mattered.

And it terrified her.

Well Reflection – When Love Looks You in the Eyes

She wasn't used to love looking her in the eyes.
She wasn't used to truth wrapped in tenderness.
She wasn't used to a man who saw her and stayed.

- What was the first moment you realized Jesus truly saw you?

- Have you ever experienced love that looked you in the eyes and stayed?

- How does it feel to know Jesus never looks away from your brokenness?

That well wasn't just a physical place.
It was the place where everything she believed about
herself came undone.

Because when Jesus sees the real you—He doesn't walk
away. He leans in.

My Moment of Truth – Being Fully Seen

For so long, I had let relationships define my worth.
My father's rejection.
The abuse in my first marriage.
The betrayal in my second.
The fear of failing my children.
The longing to be loved without having to earn it.

Even in the gentleness of this new relationship—with a
man who adored me, who loved all my children as his
own—I knew something was still missing.

Because no matter how deeply someone loves you,
If you haven't let Jesus into the broken places...
You'll always be searching for more.

I had built my life around being chosen by others—but
what I really needed was to believe I had already been
chosen by God.

Still, I resisted.
I told myself, If God really cared, He wouldn't have let me endure so much pain.

If He really saw me, why had I been left so many times?

If He loved me, why did every promise feel like it broke in my hands?

The man I loved was tangible.
He held my hand.
He wiped my tears.
He looked at me like I mattered.

But Jesus?
Sometimes He felt... far.

And even though I knew deep down that no human love could ever replace Him, I wasn't sure I was ready to trust Him again.

 "Trust in the Lord with all thine heart; and lean not unto thine own understanding." – Proverbs 3:5 (KJV)

I had spent years leaning on my own understanding—and all it led me to was more brokenness.

**This moment of truth wasn't about falling apart.
It was about finally letting Jesus into the places I'd been hiding. The places I didn't even know still hurt.**

And just like the woman at the well, when I stopped avoiding Him, when I stopped trying to change the subject, when I stood fully exposed in front of grace... He didn't turn away.

And Beloved, like me you were already chosen long before you were ever rejected.

When Jesus Confronts Your Brokenness

When Jesus spoke to the Samaritan woman, he didn't avoid her past.
He didn't sidestep the pain.
He brought it into the light—not to shame her, but to heal her.
Go, call thy husband, and come hither. John 4:16 (KJV)

He wasn't exposing her to humiliate her—He was inviting her to finally be known.

Well Reflection – Healing Requires Honesty

- What area of your life have you kept hidden because it feels too painful to face?

- Where in your life have you been pretending to be okay when you're really not?

- In what ways have you avoided God's healing by trying to stay in control or keep things buried?

What might it look like to invite Jesus into the locked-away places—honestly and completely?

I was still hiding.
Even in the love of a good man—a man who cherished me, who loved my children as his own, who dreamed of our future—I was still keeping pieces of myself hidden.

Because I was afraid that even God might walk away
If He saw too much.

But the truth is... Being accepted by someone isn't the same as being healed by Jesus.

Security isn't salvation.
Affection isn't freedom.

Only Jesus can see every broken place and call it holy ground.

He was calling me to stop building my identity around pain, to stop searching for rescue in human arms, and to start trusting the One who had never let go.

The Invitation Isn't to Shame... It's to Freedom

Jesus wasn't afraid of her truth.

He isn't afraid of yours, either.

He calls us into healing, not hiding.

This confrontation wasn't cruel.

It was the kindness of a Savior who saw every shattered piece, and still said, "Come."

The Woman at the Well – When Jesus Sees the Truth

She had been waiting for this moment her whole life— she just didn't know it.

The Samaritan woman had learned to survive by keeping her guard up.

She had been talked about, discarded, and overlooked.

She knew what it was like to be seen, but never really known.

So when this Jewish man spoke to her, she put up the only defense she had left: **walls.**

Then saith the woman of Samaria unto him, How is it that thou, being a Jew, askest drink of me, which am a woman of Samaria? For the Jews have no dealings with the Samaritans. John 4:9 (KJV)

She reminded Him of the rules.
She pointed out the reasons He shouldn't be talking to her.
She tried to deflect the conversation with logic, culture, and theology.

Because if she could keep it surface-level, maybe
He wouldn't see what she was really carrying.

But Jesus wasn't playing by her rules.

"*Jesus answered and said unto her, If thou knewest the gift of God, and who it is that saith to thee, Give me to drink; thou wouldest have asked of him,and he would have given thee living water.*" – John 4:10 (KJV)

She had spent her life knowing her place in the world— At the bottom, a Samaritan, a woman, an outcast.

And yet—He was still speaking to her like she mattered.

When Jesus Confronts What You Believe

She had grown up hearing what made her different.
Less-than, unworthy, unclean.

But now, Jesus was breaking every rule, crossing every barrier, offering her something deeper than religion: Living Water.

"The woman saith unto him, Sir, thou hast nothing to draw with, and the well is deep: from whence then hast thou that living water?" – John 4:11 (KJV)

She was still thinking in the natural.
Still looking at the bucket, the well, the physical need.
But He was reaching for her heart.

And then, He said the words that changed everything:

"Go, call thy husband, and come hither." – John 4:16 (KJV)

She froze.
She had kept the conversation safe, carefully guarded.

But now, He was reaching straight into the place she worked hardest to hide.

He knew.

"Thou hast well said, I have no husband:
For thou hast had five husbands; and he whom thou now
hast is not thy husband:
in that saidst thou truly." – John 4:17–18 (KJV)

He wasn't guessing.
He wasn't assuming.
He knew—and still, He stayed.

And like so many of us do when we feel exposed...
She tried to change the subject.

"Sir, I perceive that thou art a prophet..." – John 4:19–20
(KJV)

She shifted the focus.
She brought up theology.
She tried to keep Him at a distance.

But He was reaching straight for her soul.

Jesus Knows Who You Really Are

She had spent her whole life being defined by her
mistakes.
By what others said. By her shame.

But Jesus didn't care about where she worshiped.
He cared about whether she knew the One worthy of
worship.

"Jesus saith unto her, Woman, believe me, the hour cometh,
when ye shall neither in this mountain, nor yet at
Jerusalem, worship the Father." – John 4:21 (KJV)

Worship isn't about where you've been.
It's not about whether you belong to the "right" group.
It's about knowing the One who sees you, and still calls
you worthy.

Her heart was awakening.

"I know that Messiah cometh... when he is come, he will tell
us all things." – John 4:25 (KJV)
And then He said the words that changed everything:

"I that speak unto thee am he." – John 4:26 (KJV)

The Messiah she had been waiting for her whole life was
already standing in front of her.

Not speaking to the religious leaders. Not sitting in a temple. But right here at her well. And He came for me, too.

Facing the Ache – When Truth Finds You First

There's a moment when the mask slips.
When the performance no longer protects you.
When the conversation you tried to keep surface-level suddenly hits something raw.

And you realize...
He sees you. All of you.

Not the version you've trained the world to accept.
Not the woman who knows how to survive anything.
The real you. The broken, bruised, bleeding-you.

It's *terrifying* at first.
Because truth doesn't knock politely—it exposes what you tried to keep buried.

It puts its finger right on the place that still stings.
And suddenly, everything feels too loud, too bright, too vulnerable.

But then—something shifts.
Because you **see His face.**
And He's not flinching.
He's not walking away.
He's not shocked by what He finds.

He knew. He always knew.
And still—He came anyway.

That's when healing begins.
Not when the truth is easy to admit.
But when **Love refuses to run from it.**

You don't have to hold it together anymore.
You don't have to protect yourself from the One who
already knows.

He's not asking for your best version—He's asking for
your honest one.

And if you'll let Him... He'll take even this moment—this
ache, this unraveling—and turn it into freedom.

"And ye shall know the truth, and the truth shall make you
free." — John 8:32 (KJV)

Pour It Out: Echoes from the Well

Imagine the Samaritan woman could sit beside you right now. She's been where you are—ashamed, exhausted, misunderstood.

Write a letter from her to you.

Let her tell you what changed the day Jesus met her at the well.

Let her describe how it felt to be fully known... and still fully loved.

Let her remind you: He didn't walk away from her—and He won't walk away from you.

Then write your own response to Jesus.

Tell Him what you've been carrying.

What you've been hiding.

And ask Him to meet you at the well—right here, right now—with the truth that sets you free.

A Prayer for the One Who Feels Exposed

Lord,
You *see* them right now—no masks, no walls, no pretending.
You see the pain they've carried in silence, the shame they've hidden beneath survival, and the fear that if anyone saw the real them... they'd walk away.

But You don't. **You stay**. You reach for the places they've tried to keep locked up. You speak truth, not to wound but to free. You call them worthy when they feel anything but.

So today, I ask that You break through every barrier. Let Your love silence every lie.

Let Your presence fill the hollow spaces where rejection used to live. Teach them that being fully seen by You isn't something to fear... It's where healing begins.

"And ye shall know the truth, and the truth shall make you free." – John 8:32 (KJV)

May they choose freedom today.
Not because they've earned it, but because You already offered it.

In Jesus' name,
Amen.

Before the Storm Breaks

This chapter was a turning point in my story—not because everything was suddenly healed, but because I stopped pretending it didn't hurt.

If you're anything like me, you've spent a lot of time trying to hold it all together.

Maybe you've been the strong one. The survivor. The one who smiled when your heart was breaking.

But now... You've stood at the well.
You've let Jesus see you.

And maybe—just maybe—you're starting to believe **He isn't going anywhere.**

Part One was about being seen.

Part Two will take us into the grief we didn't choose— the kind of loss you can't fix with a Bible verse or a Sunday smile.
The kind that changes everything.

But here's what I need you to know: Even there, He is faithful.

Part Two

The Breaking Point

We all have moments where the bottom falls out—where everything we've built our lives on suddenly gives way.

This part of the journey doesn't skip the hard stuff; It invites Jesus into it.

Not just into your past, but into your grief, your fear, your questions.

Here, we don't pretend we're okay.
Here, we finally let Him meet us in the places we've been avoiding.

And maybe—just maybe...
That's where healing begins.

Chapter 4
The Death of a Good Man

When Safety Is Taken From You

I had spent years searching for love in people—trying to rewrite the story with someone who wouldn't leave, wouldn't hurt, wouldn't give up on me.

He didn't try to fix me.
He didn't run from my past.
He simply stood with me in the middle of it.

For the first time, safety felt steady.

Love felt solid.

And I started to believe I could finally stop holding my breath.

But what happens when the one person who made you feel safe... is suddenly gone?

I thought I had stopped running.
I thought I had learned to rest.
I thought I had chosen the right path.

But grief has a way of testing everything you believe.

"He healeth the broken in heart, and bindeth up their wounds." — Psalm 147:3 (KJV)

I wanted to believe the love I had found would carry me through—that this man, this good, kind, steady man, had finally made me whole.

But the moment I lost him, the ground crumbled beneath my feet.
And suddenly—every old wound I thought I had laid to rest, every scar, every fear, every whispered doubt—bled like it had never healed.

Grief doesn't just bring sorrow. It reopens the places you thought were sealed.
I thought I had stopped chasing after things that couldn't save me.

I thought I had learned that no human love could ever replace Jesus.

But when the one who made me feel safe was suddenly gone...

I didn't feel healed.
I felt like I was drowning.

Telling My Children the Unthinkable

There are moments in life that rip through time and memory—moments that never lose their sharp edges no matter how many years pass.

This was one of them.

I sat in that dimly lit room, my mother beside me—my silent strength—while the weight of the world pressed hard against my chest.

 I was holding grief in one hand and motherhood in the other, and neither felt like enough to carry what came next.

I was about to speak the words no mother should ever have to say.

How do you tell your children their father is never coming home?

How do you shatter the illusion of safety in a single breath?

My throat burned. My chest ached.
The silence between us stretched like glass—one word away from shattering.

Their eyes searched mine—wide, hopeful, afraid.
And I had no answers that could make it okay.

I whispered, "Daddy won't be able to come home... He's gone to Heaven now."

Silence. And then, from my oldest daughter—a scream. Raw, ripping, real.

"Why would he leave us?"

Her voice cracked in a way I will never forget.
It wasn't just a question.

 It was a soul crying out for stability in a world that had just come undone.

She wasn't asking about death. She was asking why heartbreak had found us again.

She collapsed into my arms, sobbing.
"Doesn't Daddy love us?
" Why would he leave?"

She couldn't understand that it wasn't his choice—that a blood clot had stolen him in a moment.

 That he didn't walk out. He was taken.

And if I'm honest... I struggled to believe it too.
Because underneath her question was my own:

Why, God?
Why again?
Why us?

I had known betrayal. I had known abandonment.
But this time... it felt like God was the one who left.

I wanted to comfort them. I wanted to speak words that could anchor us.

But the grief was louder than my faith in that moment.

All I could do was hold them.

And cry with them.

Well Reflection – Wrestling with Loss & Faith

- Have you ever felt abandoned by God in your grief?

- What questions have you been too afraid to ask Him?

- What does it mean to trust God when your world has collapsed?

"Jesus wept." — John 11:35 (KJV)

The Funeral Was a Blur

I had prepared them as best I could.
But how do you prepare a child to say goodbye to their
father forever?

The morning of the funeral came, and everything felt
heavy.
The air, the silence, even time itself seemed to slow—
thick with sorrow.

I dressed them in their best clothes, hands trembling.
I tied little shoes. Buttoned small collars.

My body moved on autopilot, but my heart was
unraveling.

Then I looked in the mirror—and barely recognized the
woman staring back.

I held their trembling hands.
I whispered words I didn't even believe myself.

"We'll get through this."
"Everything will be okay."

Well Reflection – When You're the One Holding Everyone Together

- Have you ever whispered words to comfort others that you didn't fully believe yourself?

- Have you ever carried a strength you didn't feel, just to protect those who needed you?

- What would it look like to let God hold you—while you hold everyone else?

"He giveth power to the faint; and to them that have no might he increaseth strength." — Isaiah 40:29 (KJV)

But inside, I wasn't sure we would.
Inside, I was holding myself together by sheer will.

Because if I let go—if I stopped moving, stopped breathing, even for a second—I knew I would crumble right in front of them.

We stood together at the graveside—too young to understand the full weight of this loss, but too heartbroken to ignore it.

My five-year-old son clutched my hand so tightly I lost feeling in my fingers.
His little body shook, but he didn't speak a word.
He didn't have to. The silence said everything.

My oldest daughter held her little sister's hand. Tears pooled but didn't fall.

Her lips were pressed tight. Her jaw clenched—not in defiance, but in fierce protection.

She was trying to be strong, to be brave.

To shield her siblings from a world that had just proven it couldn't be trusted.

Even in her heartbreak, she was determined not to let them feel alone.

And then—the moment I had dreaded most.

"For dust thou art, and unto dust shalt thou return." —
Genesis 3:19 (KJV)

The casket was lowered.
The dirt was shoveled.
And just like that... he was gone.

Gone, like my daughter had been.
Gone, like every sense of safety I had ever clung to.

As I stood there beside his grave—children trembling at my side, my heart split open with sorrow—another scene came to mind.

The quiet moments when he stood beside me at my Daughter's grave. Holidays, birthdays, ordinary days when grief came uninvited.

He would place his hand gently on my back in silent support as I knelt to lay flowers.

Sometimes, he'd whisper, "She can be mine too."

And I believed him. He loved her and honored her memory like she was his own.

So on that day, as the earth swallowed the last piece of him we could touch, I whispered through tears,

"Please find her. Hug her for me. Tell her how much Mommy misses her."

And somehow, in that moment, Heaven felt closer.

Not just because he was there—but because I knew he'd carry my love into eternity.
And wrap it around the daughter I lost.

He would make sure she felt all the love I had longed to give her.

When You're the One Left Behind

Grief didn't ask for permission.
It didn't come in gently.
It stormed in—wild and unrelenting—and I was left to pick
up the pieces while trying to stay strong for my kids.

*There's a strange kind of loneliness that settles in when the
one person who understood your world is suddenly gone.*

He was the only one who knew our inside jokes.
The only one who remembered every detail of the
pregnancies.

The way I cried during Hallmark movies...
And laughed too loud at the wrong times.
He knew the real me—flawed, fiery, fierce—and loved me
anyway.

And *now*... He was *gone*.

I kept waiting for someone to tell me how to breathe again.

How to carry his memory without collapsing under the weight of it.

How to show up for my children when I barely had the strength to crawl out of bed.

They weren't toddlers anymore—my youngest was four, old enough to remember, old enough to ask questions I didn't know how to answer.

How do you help a grieving child fall asleep when the sound of your own sobs break through the lullabies?

The world didn't pause for our pain.

The bills still came.

The dishes still piled up.

Life kept moving—even when I didn't want it to.

And through it all, a whisper stirred in my spirit—quiet, steady, stubborn:

"*You're not alone.*" Even when I felt like I was.

When Anger Joins the Grief

Grief doesn't follow a script. It crashes into you—wild and uninvited—and just when you think the worst has passed, something deeper starts to rise: Anger.

Not the kind that yells.
The kind that simmers.
It whispers in the quiet moments:

"Why would God let this happen?"

"How could this be part of any good plan?"

I wasn't angry at him. I knew he didn't choose to leave.
But I was angry at the weight he left me to carry.
Angry that I had to be strong for everyone else.
Angry that, once again, I was alone in the ruins of another loss.

I wanted to believe that God was still good.
But I couldn't see how. Not in this.

"My God, my God, why hast thou forsaken me?" —
Matthew 27:46 (KJV)

That verse haunted me.

Because I felt it, too—forsaken.

I looked at my grieving children.

Our quiet home.

My broken heart.

And I wondered how any of this could possibly lead to something good.

But even in my fury—God didn't leave.

He didn't rebuke my questions.
He didn't run from my rage.
He didn't disappear when I did.

He remained.
He leaned in.
He let me scream, weep, rage, collapse.
And He didn't flinch.

Because His love isn't afraid of our honesty.

Even in the silence, I could still sense His presence.
Not loud, not obvious, but steady.

"Whither shall I go from thy spirit? or whither shall I flee from thy presence?" — Psalm 139:7 (KJV)

Well Reflection – When Anger Fills the Empty Places

Anger isn't the opposite of faith.

It's what happens when faith feels like it's burning at both ends.

- Have you ever felt angry at God for how your life unfolded?

- What would it look like to bring your anger to Him instead of hiding it?

- Have you given yourself permission to feel it... and still be loved?

    "The Lord is nigh unto them that are of a broken heart; and saveth such as be of a contrite spirit." — *Psalm 34:18 (KJV)*

When Grief Changes Your Identity

Grief doesn't just break your heart—it reshapes
everything you thought you were.
I didn't recognize myself anymore.
Not just because of the tears or the exhaustion—but
because I didn't know how to be me without him.

I wasn't just mourning his death.
I was mourning the version of myself that existed when
he was still alive.
The woman who felt safe.
The woman who felt seen.
The woman who finally believed
She didn't have to carry it all alone.

And now?
She was gone too.

I became a solo parent.

A widow, a woman who had tasted love and security—and
now had to explain its absence to her children every
single day.

And underneath the weight of grief, titles, and trauma, a
quiet question echoed in my soul:

Who am I now?

"I will not leave you comfortless: I will come to you."
— John 14:18 (KJV)

I didn't feel comforted.
I felt lost.
Not just emotionally—but spiritually.

Like the woman I had become with him was buried beneath the weight of what I had lost.

But even in the dark, something inside me whispered:

"This isn't the end of your story."

Grief had shattered my identity.
But God wasn't afraid of what was left behind.

He was gently picking up the pieces—even the ones I didn't know how to name.

Well Reflection – When Grief Steals Who You Thought You Were

Grief doesn't just take someone you love. It takes the version of yourself that existed when they were still here.

- How has grief changed the way you see yourself?

- What identity have you struggled to reclaim in the aftermath of loss?

"Fear thou not; for I am with thee: be not dismayed; for I am thy God..." — Isaiah 41:10 (KJV)

Breathing through the Breakdown

There's a grief so deep it silences even your prayers.
That was the place I found myself—not because I didn't believe in God, but because I couldn't feel Him anymore.

I was grieving a man, but I was also grieving stability, safety, and hope.
I was grieving what could have been. What we were building. What my heart had finally dared to trust.

And in that hollow space, where the echo of loss rang louder than truth—faith didn't feel like enough.

I kept asking questions I never thought I'd ask:

Why would You let this happen now?

Why give my children a sense of peace—only to take it away?

Why allow me to feel chosen—only to be left again?

I wasn't proud of those questions. But they were real.

And I've learned since then—God doesn't require silence from our sorrow.
He welcomes it.

"The Lord is nigh unto them that are of a broken heart; and saveth such as be of a contrite spirit." —
Psalm 34:18 (KJV)

I didn't feel Him in loud, miraculous ways.
But there were moments—a *quiet nudge, a soft whisper, a* sudden breath of *peace*—that reminded me He *was still there*.

It didn't erase the ache.
But it gave me just enough to take the next breath.

To get out of bed.
To hold my children a little tighter.

And sometimes, that's all faith needs to do.
Not explain, not fix, just stay.

I was still walking through the ache, still carrying questions that didn't have answers.
But something quiet had begun to shift.

I wasn't shouting anymore—I was listening.
And in that listening, I started to realize that even when God felt silent...
He *had never stopped being present*.

Faith doesn't mean you never wrestle. It means you keep holding on, even when the answers haven't come yet.

- What questions have you been holding back from God out of fear or shame?

- What would it look like to bring them to Him—right in the middle of your ache?

"Casting all your care upon him; for he careth for you." — 1 Peter 5:7 (KJV)

I wasn't healed yet.
I didn't feel strong. But I was still His.
And somehow, even when I had nothing left to give—He never stopped holding me.

That's the kind of love that carries you through the unthinkable.

Not the kind that avoids the storm—but the kind that holds your hand through every wave.

The Woman Who Knew the Ache of Being Left Behind

I wonder what kind of grief the Samaritan woman buried
beneath her skin.

We talk about her string of failed relationships, her
shame, her isolation—but rarely do we pause to consider
her losses.

Because maybe it wasn't just about the husbands.
Maybe it was about the *hopes* that died with each one.
Maybe it was about the love she thought would last—
Only to be left with nothing but whispers and wounds.

And truthfully—it's likely she was a widow, or abandoned.
Because in her time, a woman couldn't initiate divorce
easily.
Men held the power to walk away.
Women didn't.

So if she had been through five husbands,
It's possible she didn't leave them—they left her.
By death.
By rejection.
By choices she never got to make.

No wonder she was tired.
No wonder she came to the well in the heat of the day—
avoiding the stares, avoiding the shame.

She didn't show up that day looking for Jesus.
She showed up because she needed water.
She was just trying to survive.
Like I was.

And when Jesus met her there, He didn't ask her to perform.
He didn't demand she explain her pain. He simply acknowledged it.

"You are right in saying, 'I have no husband'; for you have had five husbands, and the one you now have is not your husband" — (John 4:17-18).

That wasn't condemnation. That was recognition.

It was Jesus saying:
I see what life has taken from you.
I see the pieces you're carrying.
I see how tired you are of surviving.

And I get it now.

Because I wasn't looking for Him either.
I was just trying to hold it together.
Trying to raise babies in the middle of heartbreak.
Trying to breathe when grief pressed hard on my chest.

But He met me, too.
Right in the middle of the ache.
And He didn't turn away from my pain. He stayed.

"The Lord also will be a refuge for the oppressed, a refuge in times of trouble." — Psalm 9:9 (KJV)

Facing the Ache – When Loss Redefines Everything

Grief doesn't just visit you. It rewrites you without warning, without permission.

One moment, you're doing life with someone who knows your story—the next, you're staring into the silence they left behind.
And it's not just their absence that undoes you.
It's the way your identity fractures in the fallout.

You used to be a wife, a partner, a co-parent.
A woman building something sacred with someone you trusted.

Now... You're something else, someone else.
But you didn't choose this version of you.
The one who once felt steady Now wakes to uncertainty.

The one who once stood beside someone is suddenly standing alone.
Not because she failed—but because loss forced her into a life she never asked for.

You try to keep going.
For the kids. For the bills.
For the expectations that never pause—even when your world has.

But inside, you feel like a stranger to yourself.
Not broken.
Not destroyed.
Just... undone.

And that's where Jesus meets you.
Not once you're whole again—but in the unraveling.

In the slow, sacred space where you stop trying to be the woman you were and start discovering who you are.

Not forgotten.
Not forsaken.
Not invisible.

Just held.
Right here.
In the ache.

"I will not leave you comfortless: I will come to you." — John 14:18 (KJV)

Pour It Out – Journaling Through the Ache

Grief can make you feel like you've lost not only someone you loved—but the version of yourself that existed when they were still here.

Use this space to pour out what's been buried deep:

Who were you before this loss—and who are you now?

What pieces of yourself have been the hardest to carry forward?

Where do you still feel "undone"... and where might God be meeting you in that very place?

Write a letter to the person you lost.

What do you wish they knew? What do you still carry?

Let the tears fall.
Let the silence speak.
Let the ache be honest.

And trust that God can hold every word—even the ones you're not ready to say out loud.

A Prayer for the One Still Carrying What Feels Unbearable

Lord,
You see the one reading these words through tears.
The one who feels like the life she knew has shattered beyond repair.

She may not even know how she got here—only that everything feels heavier now.
Quieter.
Lonelier.

Maybe she's tried to stay strong for everyone else.
Maybe she's tucked her grief behind a smile
Because falling apart never felt like an option.

But You know the truth behind the silence.
You see the way her heart aches.
You see the way her chest tightens
Every time she tries to explain something that has no words.

She doesn't need quick answers.
She needs to **know she's not alone in this**.

So meet her here, Lord—right here, in the pain she hasn't
fully named.

In the nights when sleep won't come.
In the moments when the world expects her to move on,
but she still feels stuck.

Wrap Your presence around her like a weighted blanket.
Not to take the ache away all at once—but to remind her
she's still held in the middle of it.

Whisper to her the truth she's afraid to believe:
That she is not broken beyond repair.

That healing doesn't mean forgetting.
And that You haven't left—not for a moment.

Amen.

Chapter 5

The Marriage Fear Built

When Fear Feels Like Faith

I didn't marry him because I was in love.
I married him because I was afraid.
Afraid of raising my kids alone. Afraid of what loneliness might do to me.
Afraid that I'd never feel secure again.

He seemed like a safe choice—stable, employed, a father with full custody of his daughter.

On paper, it looked like provision. But brokenness doesn't read résumés. Grief doesn't care how good someone looks on paper.

And fear? Fear can dress up like wisdom when your heart is tired.

I didn't realize I was choosing comfort over calling.
I was trying to outrun pain by rebuilding too quickly.
And for a while... I told myself it was working.

We were two single parents trying to make life work.
We blended our households.
We showed up at school events. We made dinners, paid bills, and took turns.

But behind the doors of that "new start," something unspoken lived. Something that crept in quietly—until it no longer could be ignored.

When Redemption Feels Out of Reach

There's a specific kind of shame that sets in when you realize you've made another mistake—not the loud kind others point to, but the quiet ache that whispers, "You should've known better."

I had already lost so much. And instead of healing, I tried to rebuild my life on the thinnest foundation—grief, survival, fear. And now that foundation was crumbling. I felt like I had failed again. Not just myself. Not just my children.
But even my relationship with God.

How could I keep saying I trusted Him and end up here—again?

There were nights I buried my face in my pillow, wondering if God had given up on me.
Wondering if maybe I had finally reached the point where grace didn't apply to me anymore.

But here's what I've learned: Redemption doesn't wait for our story to get pretty.

It meets us in the middle of the mess.

Jesus doesn't stand at a distance, waiting for us to clean up the wreckage—He walks straight into it, with healing in His hands.

I wasn't too far gone. I was just in the middle of the story.

And so are you.

When God Interrupts the Pattern

It's one thing to walk away from pain—it's another to walk into healing.

After I left that marriage, I didn't feel immediately restored.
I felt exhausted, embarrassed, ashamed that I had made another mistake.

But God didn't meet me with judgment. He met me with mercy.

He didn't scold me for running ahead of Him—He simply stood where I had stopped,
Patient and present, waiting for me to turn around.

"And thine ears shall hear a word behind thee, saying, This is the way, walk ye in it..." — Isaiah 30:21 (KJV)

I had been walking in circles— From man to man, from fear to fear, from well to well that never satisfied.

But **God was offering something different**.
Not a quick fix.

Not a new relationship.
But a deeper healing.
The kind of healing that asks you to stop pretending.
The kind that begins with truth.

And the truth was—I hadn't just married a broken man.
I had brought my own brokenness into that marriage, too.

I had let fear drive the decision.
I had let grief set the timeline.
I had trusted a person to do what only Jesus could.

That was the pattern.

But God was about to interrupt it.

Well Reflection – When You Finally See the Pattern

Have you ever recognized a cycle in your life—a repeated decision made from fear, loneliness, or survival?

Maybe you've walked away from something broken, only to find yourself drawn to the same kind of brokenness again.

It's not because you're weak— It's because wounded hearts often reach for what feels familiar.

- But what if God is trying to interrupt the pattern?

- What behaviors or relationships have you repeated, hoping for a different result?

- What false comforts have you leaned on to soothe old wounds?

- What would it look like to invite Jesus into that cycle—and ask Him to break it?

"The Lord is gracious, and full of compassion; slow to anger, and of great mercy." — Psalm 145:8 (KJV)

The Woman at the Well – Returning to Broken Wells

The Samaritan woman had been through five husbands.
And the man she was with now? He wasn't even her
husband.

To us, that might sound like a series of bad choices.
But in her time, it likely told a different story.

Women in ancient Jewish culture couldn't simply file for
divorce. Marriage and divorce were controlled by men—
and often, women were dismissed for reasons as simple
as burning a meal or not bearing children.

Each failed marriage may not have been her decision at
all.
It's entirely possible she had been abandoned, widowed,
or discarded—again and again.

She didn't just carry the pain of rejection.
She carried the cultural shame of being considered
unworthy, unlovable, unchosen.

And so she came to the well alone.
In the heat of the day—when no one else would be there.
Not because it was convenient, but because it was safer
than the stares and whispers.

She wasn't just tired of drawing water.
She was tired of drawing from relationships that never
truly filled her.

And maybe... that's where I found myself too.

I wasn't chasing men for love—I was chasing relief, security, rescue.

But every time I returned to that kind of well, I left more empty than when I came.

Until one day...
Jesus was there—sitting at the edge of that very pattern.

Waiting.

Waiting for her to stop repeating the cycle.
Waiting for her to realize she didn't need another man.

She needed the Messiah.

"Whosoever drinketh of this water shall thirst again: But whosoever drinketh of the water that I shall give him shall never thirst..." — John 4:13–14 (KJV)

When God Calls You Out of the Cycle

I didn't just need to leave a broken marriage—I needed to leave the mindset that kept leading me into broken ones.

God wasn't trying to punish me. He was trying to heal me.

He was calling me to stop building my future around people...And start rebuilding it around Him.

But it didn't happen overnight.

It happened in layers.

In questions. In quiet, surrendered moments where I finally asked:

"God, what do You want to heal in me?"

"Create in me a clean heart, O God; and renew a right spirit within me." — Psalm 51:10 (KJV)

He wasn't after my perfection. He was after my participation.

He was asking me to stop numbing my pain with people—and start *handing it to the One who could redeem it.*

"With joy shall ye draw water out of the wells of salvation." — Isaiah 12:3 (KJV)

When the Pain Turns Inward – The Lies Shame Tells

It wasn't just the marriage that broke.
It was the version of me I had tried to become.

The one who thought she had to hold it all together.
The one who believed being strong meant never admitting regret.

The one who smiled through disappointment because honesty felt too costly.

But you can't outrun what you refuse to feel.
Eventually... the cracks spread.

Shame doesn't always shout.
Sometimes, it whispers in your most vulnerable moments:

"This is what you deserve."

"No one will take you seriously now."

"You're too broken to be used."

And if you're not careful, you start agreeing with it.

I wasn't just grieving another failed relationship—I was grieving the version of myself I had hoped would finally get it right.

I thought I had learned the lessons.

I thought I had changed.

But standing in the aftermath, I couldn't help but wonder if something was wrong with me.

"He restoreth my soul: he leadeth me in the paths of righteousness for his name's sake." — Psalm 23:3 (KJV)

But shame is a liar. It turns survival into self-blame. It turns grief into guilt.

And it silences the truth:

That even in the mess, God is still writing a story worth telling.

Well Reflection — When Shame Becomes the Loudest Voice

- What silent agreements have you made with shame—statements you've repeated in your mind that were never from God?

- How has shame shaped the way you see yourself when no one's watching?

- What would it take to stop measuring your worth by what you've been through—and start receiving God's truth about who you are?

"There is therefore now no condemnation to them which are in Christ Jesus..." — Romans 8:1 (KJV)

When Forgiveness Begins With You

I wanted to blame him for everything.
For the lies, the drinking, for making me believe we could build something that would last.

But the truth?
I had brought wounds into that marriage, too.
And I had expected another human being to do what only God could—make me feel whole again.

I thought forgiveness meant excusing what he did.

But what God showed me was something deeper: forgiveness wasn't just about releasing him—it was about releasing me.

Letting go of the anger I was drinking like poison.

Letting go of the shame that whispered, *"This is all your fault."*

"Let all bitterness, and wrath, and anger, and clamour, and evil speaking, be put away from you... and be ye kind one to another, tenderhearted, forgiving one another, even as God for Christ's sake hath forgiven you." — Ephesians 4:31–32 (KJV)

Forgiveness doesn't say, "It was okay."
It says, "I'm not carrying this anymore."

I didn't want to stay bitter.
I didn't want to stay stuck.
And I definitely didn't want to bring the same wounds
into the next season of my life.
So I started praying for him.
Not because I felt like it.

But because I needed to be free.

Well Reflection – When Letting Go Sets You Free

- Who have you been silently holding responsible for your pain—even if you've never said it out loud?

- What weight have you carried in your heart that you were never meant to hold?

- Could it be that forgiveness isn't about forgetting— but about freeing yourself to heal?

"And when ye stand praying, forgive, if ye have ought against any..." — Mark 11:25 (KJV)

When God Uses the Breaking to Bring You Back

Leaving wasn't the end of the story—it was the beginning of surrender.
I thought I had already been broken.
But this time, the breaking felt different.

It wasn't just loss—it was revelation.

It was the moment I stopped blaming the world for my wounds and started letting God touch the parts of me I had hidden.

The grief of what I thought my life would be...
The shame of what I settled for...
The fear that maybe I wasn't meant to experience lasting love...

God saw it all..

"The Lord is nigh unto them that are of a broken heart; and saveth such as be of a contrite spirit." — Psalm 34:18 (KJV)

This wasn't the life I had prayed for.
It wasn't the love I had dreamed of.

But it was the **place where I finally stopped striving—and started trusting.**

I didn't need another man to rescue me.

I needed to be rescued from the lies I believed about myself.

And Jesus? He met me in that breaking.

He didn't ask me to clean up the mess first.
He simply whispered: "I'm still here. And I'm not done with your story."

Well Reflection – When the Breaking Becomes the Turning

- Have you mistaken survival for healing—holding yourself together when God was actually inviting you to fall into His arms?

- What have you been trying to fix with your own hands that God is asking you to surrender completely?

- If you believed the breaking wasn't a punishment but an invitation—how would it change the way you see your story?

"Humble yourselves therefore under the mighty hand of God, that he may exalt you in due time: Casting all your care upon him; for he careth for you." — 1 Peter 5:6-7 (KJV)

When Grace Starts to Build Something New

There's something sacred about starting over—not from a place of desperation, but from a place of surrender.

This time, I wasn't looking for someone to save me. I was letting Jesus rebuild me. Little by little, He began to mend what I thought was too broken. Not with flashy miracles or overnight fixes—but through quiet moments of healing.

He sent friendships that spoke life over me.
He stirred dreams in me that I had buried under survival.
He began to remind me who I was... and who I wasn't.

"And I will give them a heart to know me, that I am the Lord: and they shall be my people, and I will be their God: for they shall return unto me with their whole heart." — Jeremiah 24:7 (KJV)

I didn't need to be rescued. I needed to be restored.
I didn't need to go back. I needed to go deeper.

And that's exactly what grace did—it met me in the ruins and started drawing up blueprints for something new.

"And they that shall be of thee shall build the old waste places: thou shalt raise up the foundations of many generations; and thou shalt be called, The repairer of the breach..." — Isaiah 58:12 (KJV)

When God Heals What You Didn't Know Was Broken

It's easy to focus on the obvious wounds—the ones that bleed loud.
The ones others can see.

But some of the most dangerous wounds are the ones that stay hidden.

Buried beneath "I'm fine."

Buried beneath busyness, performance, and pretending.

I didn't know how deep my fear of abandonment ran— until I was alone again.

I didn't know how much I'd been trying to earn love—until no one was left to applaud the effort.

I didn't know how far I had drifted from my worth— until Jesus met me in the quiet and said, "*Daughter...I never asked you to prove anything.*"

"Yea, I have loved thee with an everlasting love: therefore with lovingkindness have I drawn thee." — Jeremiah 31:3 (KJV)

God didn't just want to heal the wounds of a decision driven by fear.

He wanted to heal the part of me that thought love had to be earned.

He wanted to show me that the deepest wells of healing aren't found in people. They're found in His presence.

Well Reflection – What's Hiding Beneath the Surface?

- What fears have shaped your past decisions, even when you thought you were choosing wisely?

- Where have you traded authenticity for acceptance—presenting strength while silently breaking inside?

- What would it look like to trust God with the version of you that's still scared to be fully seen?

"The Lord is good, a strong hold in the day of trouble; and he knoweth them that trust in him." — Nahum 1:7 (KJV)

When the Jar Finally Drops

The Samaritan woman didn't just leave a man or a mindset behind—she left her jar.

That symbol of survival. That representation of shame. *That burden she carried every day, just to keep going. And when she met Jesus—she let it go.*

I carried that jar too.
Every broken choice.
Every silent tear.
Every false identity I believed because I thought that's all I deserved.

But when grace met me in the wilderness of my worst decisions—when Jesus didn't turn away from the weight I held—I realized something powerful:

I *didn't have to carry it anymore.*

Because freedom doesn't come when we get it all right. It comes when we finally admit—we never could.

It comes when we hand the jar over...
And let Living Water fill the places we once tried to fill on our own.

"If the Son therefore shall make you free, ye shall be free indeed." — John 8:36 (KJV)

Face the Ache – When the Healing Begins in the Silence

There's a quiet ache that shows up after the dust settles.
After the decisions have been made.
After the noise fades and you're left alone with your thoughts.

Strong on the outside—but something inside still stings.

It's the ache of knowing you walked away because you had to...
And yet, something in you still longs for what should have been different.
It's the ache of realizing too late where the pattern began—and wishing you'd seen it sooner.

Maybe you didn't turn your back on God.
Maybe you just tried to move forward without waiting for Him.

And when everything fell apart, it wasn't His judgment you feared—it was that familiar whisper of shame:

"How did I end up here again?"

But this is where God meets you.
Not at the end of your strength, but right there in the pause—in the in-between.

In the ache that lingers after the pretending stops.

He doesn't ask for explanations.

He doesn't wait for you to fix it.
He just steps in, right into the middle of what you still don't have words for, and says: "

I see you.

I still choose you.

I never stopped."

You don't have to climb your way back to worthiness.
You don't have to prove you're ready for healing.

This—right here, right now—is where the turning begins.

"Being confident of this very thing, that he which hath begun a good work in you will perform it until the day of Jesus Christ." — Philippians 1:6 (KJV)

Pour It Out – A Letter from the Woman with the Jar

Write a letter to the version of yourself who settled—the one who believed fear was safer than faith.

The one who made compromises just to feel chosen. The one who kept holding it together, even when everything inside was unraveling.

Speak gently to her.
Remind her she was doing the best she could with what she knew.
Let her know she is seen now—not for her mistakes, but for her courage to keep going.

Then write a letter from Jesus to that same version of you.
Let His words wash over her shame.

 Let Him call her by her real name—not broken, not too late—but beloved.

Let Him remind her that she doesn't have to earn His love. She only has to receive it.

"For I know the thoughts that I think toward you, saith the Lord, thoughts of peace, and not of evil, to give you an expected end." — Jeremiah 29:11 (KJV)

A Prayer for the One Who Settled Out of Fear

Lord,
You see the one who didn't say "yes" from joy, but from the ache of not wanting to be alone.
The **one who mistook survival for strength, and silence for peace.**
The one **who hoped stability would be enough, even when her heart whispered that something was missing.**

You know how hard she tried—to make it work, to make it holy, to make it feel like love.

You saw the tears she hid behind responsibility.
You heard the prayers she whispered in rooms that felt too quiet.
You felt the weight of her pretending—and You never turned away.

You didn't shame her for choosing what felt safe.
You didn't abandon her when she ran ahead.

You stood in the shadows of her disappointment, ready to rebuild from the rubble.

So today, meet her here—In the space between regret and hope.
In the place where she's learning to forgive herself.
In the middle of what she let go... and what she's still afraid to believe is possible.

Remind her that she is not disqualified.
Not forgotten.

Not too late to be held by love that doesn't fail.

Speak truth where shame still echoes.
Bring healing where fear once drove her choices.
Pour Your grace over every piece she thought was too messy to matter.

And when she finally lets go of the jar—the jar of striving, of settling, of saving herself—let Living Water rush in.
Let freedom rise.
Let peace settle deep.

Because You're not just restoring what was broken—you're revealing what was beautiful all along.

In Jesus' name,
Amen.

Chapter 6
The Murder Call

When the Phone Rings with the Unthinkable

It had been *years since I left him.*
Years since I walked out of that house, pregnant and broken, *determined never to look back.*

I had rebuilt, I had healed—or at least I thought I had.

But then came the call.
The kind that freezes time.
The kind that drops a weight on your chest so heavy, you forget how to breathe.

"He's gone."

Those words shouldn't have shaken me.
He hadn't been part of my life for a long time.
But they did.

Because this wasn't just anyone.

This was the man who fathered my first child.

The man who beat me while I carried life inside me.
The man who locked the doors, raised his fists, and left me bleeding—but also the man I once loved.

 The man I thought I had escaped for good.

117

And now he was dead.
Murdered by his cellmate in a prison cell.
On the anniversary of our daughter's birth—the one we
lost to SIDS.

What are the odds?
What kind of cosmic pain is that?
It felt cruel.

 Like grief had boomeranged back around just to remind
me of everything I thought I had buried.

I didn't know how to process it.
I wasn't mourning *him*, exactly.
I was mourning the years I lost trying to fix what was
never mine to fix.
I was mourning the little girl he never got to raise.
The innocence that never returned after the abuse.

The safety I never got to reclaim in his presence. And
most of all, I was mourning the version of me that still
flinched when I heard his name.

Because even in death, he held power I hadn't realized I
had never taken back.

Well Reflection – When Grief Reopens Old Wounds

Some losses don't bring peace.

They reopen chapters you thought were closed.

- What part of your past still holds a kind of power over you, even after all these years?

- Have you ever been caught off guard by grief that you thought you had already healed from?

- What would it look like to reclaim the pieces of yourself that were stolen in that season?

"He has sent me to bind up the brokenhearted, to proclaim liberty to the captives..." — Isaiah 61:1

Telling My Daughter Her Father Was Dead

She was grown now.
Living in the city.
Full of fire and independence—the very things I once
begged God to give her when she was just a girl I held
close through the wreckage.

I didn't expect the moment to come so suddenly.
But when it did, I knew I had to be the one to tell her.

Even if the words felt like glass in my mouth.
I called her.

My voice steady on the outside.
 But unraveling on the inside.

"Baby... I need to tell you something."
She was quiet.
Alert.

She knew me well enough to hear the tension behind my
words.

**"Your biological father...he's gone. He was killed. In
prison."**

I held my breath on the other end of the line.

Waited for the tears.
Waited for the anger.
Waited for anything.
But she didn't flinch.

She acted unfazed—cool, calm, collected.
Just like I had taught her to be.

But we both knew the truth.

Because her silence wasn't empty.

It was full of all the things we never said. I had spent her childhood building a wall between her and the pain that could have destroyed her.

I told her just enough to protect her, and not a word more.

"You're too good to be part of that," I used to say.
"His life is too much of a mess.
You deserve better."
And she believed me.

I did everything I could to make sure she wouldn't carry the weight of his brokenness.

That his story wouldn't shape hers.

That the legacy of addiction, violence, and chaos would end with me.

But this time—this one final time—I couldn't protect her.

The chapter was closed.
His part of our story—done.
And all I could do was let her sit in that quiet, final sentence.

Not because she loved him.
Not because she missed him.
*But because **even unspoken grief has a sound.***
And in that moment, we both heard it.

Well Reflection – The Silence Between Generations

Sometimes, the loudest grief is the kind that's never spoken.

- What pain have you protected others from by staying silent?

- Have you ever inherited grief that wasn't fully explained to you?

- What would it look like to break the cycle of silence without breaking your own heart?

When Closure Isn't the Same as Healing

I thought I'd feel something different when he died.
Relief, maybe.
A sense of justice.

An invisible door finally closing on a chapter I never wanted to reread.

But instead, there was... nothing.
Not at first. Just a hollow ache that echoed louder than I expected.

Because even when someone doesn't deserve a place in your future, their impact on your past still lingers.

I wasn't mourning a love lost—I was grieving what that chapter of my life took from me.

The trust it shattered.

The woman it broke.
The parts of me that I had to bury just to survive.

And in some strange, quiet way... I was also grieving the finality.

The fact that there would never be a reckoning.
No apology, no answers, no clean ending.
Just a violent exit on the anniversary of the child we lost.

Some stories don't wrap up with neat bows or clear answers.

Sometimes the pain is real, the ending is messy, and healing feels delayed.

- Have you ever waited for an apology that never came?

- Are there parts of your past that still feel unfinished or unanswered?

- Could freedom begin if you released the need for a final word?

"You keep track of all my sorrows. You have collected all my tears in Your bottle. You have recorded each one in Your book." — Psalm 56:8 (NLT)

I had spent so long trying not to hate him, trying to forgive what felt unforgivable, trying to protect my Daughter from his legacy.

And now—the man who once terrorized my world was just... gone.

Reduced to a headline, a file, a whisper.

And still—it stirred something in me.
A reminder that some grief doesn't come from love.
It comes from what should have never happened in the first place.

And maybe what haunted me most wasn't how he died—but the fact that his story had no redemption in it.

No turning point.
No moment of clarity or grace.
Just a slow unraveling that ended in a prison cell… and a death no one saw coming.

He let the grief break him.
He let the pain define him.
And in that final chapter, I saw what could've become of me—if I had stayed bitter.

If I had never let God heal me.

If I had let tragedy write the rest of my story.

But I made a choice to live.

To break the pattern.
To let grief shape me, but not destroy me.

His story ended in a prison.
Mine didn't have to.

Well Reflection – When Their Story Ends but Yours Keeps Going

Some stories don't get a happy ending—at least not here on earth.

- Have you ever mourned a person more for who they could've been than who they were?

- Have you ever seen someone's life become a warning instead of a testimony?

- What choices are you making today to live a different ending?

"Be not overcome of evil, but overcome evil with good." –
Romans 12:21 (KJV

The Woman Whose Past Could Have Defined Her

I think about her sometimes—the Samaritan woman at the well. Not the version we often hear about in sermons... But the real woman.

The one who knew what it felt like to be avoided, misunderstood, labeled by the worst parts of her story. The one who had been passed from man to man like she was disposable.

The one who walked to the well in the heat of the day— not because it was convenient, but because shame had rearranged her entire life. And I wonder if she felt like I did that day.

Carrying pain that had no words. Wounds that had never truly healed.
Grief buried under years of survival.

She wasn't looking for healing.
She was just trying to make it to the next day.
Just like I had been. Just like I was again when that phone call came and reopened a wound I thought was scarred over. And yet, Jesus met her there.

Not at the temple.
Not at the altar.
Not when she had it all together.

He met her in the middle of her pain.
In the middle of her shame.
In the middle of the life she thought disqualified her.
And He didn't flinch

He didn't condemn her.
He didn't shame her.
He simply spoke truth that pierced through every defense
she had built.

He named her pain.
He acknowledged her story.
And He offered her something better than survival—
Living Water.

When I reflect on how my past came crashing back into
my life through a single phone call, I see now what Jesus
was doing with me too.

He was meeting me again at the well.

**Not to remind me of who I used to be—but to remind me of
who I am now.**
Redeemed, rescued, loved.

Not because I did everything right.
*But because He never stopped coming for me—even when I
thought the story was over.*

*"Jesus answered and said unto her, Whosoever drinketh of
this water shall thirst again: But whosoever drinketh of the
water that I shall give him shall never thirst..." — John 4:13–
14 (KJV)*

Facing the Ache – When the Past Still Echoes

Have you ever thought a chapter of your life was closed—
only for grief to crack it open again?

Maybe you've done the work.

You've gone to therapy.
You've prayed.
You've forgiven.
You've moved forward...

But then something triggers it.
A phone call, a date, a memory.
And suddenly, you're back in the ache like no time has
passed at all.

It doesn't mean you've failed.
It means you're human.

Sometimes, healing comes in layers.
Sometimes, the pain shows up again not to haunt you—
But to invite you to go even deeper with God than you did
before.

Let Him into the places that still sting.
Let Him tend to the wounds that weren't as closed as
you thought.
You're not back where you started.
You're being refined.

"He shall sit as a refiner and purifier of silver..." — Malachi
3:3 (KJV)

Pour It Out – When the Grief Still Lingers

This is your moment to stop pretending it didn't hurt.

The years you lost trying to hold it all together.
The silence you carried so no one would worry.

The day they left—whether by choice, by force, or by death—and the ache that still hasn't let you go.

Write from that place.

From the part of you that still flinches at the sound of their name.

From the memories you've tried to bury but that keep clawing their way back.

From the questions no one ever answered—and maybe never will.

Let it spill.

The heartbreak you minimized.

The rage you swallowed.
The grief that rises without warning, even after all this time.

Tell Jesus the truth.

Not the polished version.
Not the church words.
But the raw, bleeding truth from the part of you that still feels unfinished.

Tell Him what they did.
What you lost.
What still feels broken.

And then ask Him—not just to listen, but to speak.

To speak to the part of you that's been stuck in survival mode.

To the soul that's tired of pretending it's already okay.

To the woman who's wondering if healing could ever *really* be for her.

Let Him meet you at the well—not to erase what happened, but to fill what was emptied.

You are not too far gone. You are not too broken. And this story isn't finished.

"He restoreth my soul..." — Psalm 23:3 (KJV)

A Prayer for the One Who's Still Healing from What Wasn't Fair

Lord,
You see her.
The woman reading this who has carried more than her share of sorrow.
The one who kept going when it would've been easier to quit.
The **one who put on a brave face because falling apart felt too risky.**

You know the weight she still holds.
The trauma she never asked for.
The moments that stole her breath—and the silence that followed.

She's done the best she could.
But she's tired, Lord.

Tired of pretending she's over it.
Tired of feeling like she has to be "fine" just to be accepted.
Tired of wondering if the pain she carries will ever fully lift.

So come close, Jesus.

Meet her in the places no one else sees.
In the ache she pushes past just to function.
In the questions that still go unanswered.
In the memories that rise without warning.

Wrap her in the kind of love that doesn't flinch.
The kind that doesn't need her to be okay first.

Let her breathe again.
Not because everything makes sense, but because she
knows she's not alone in it anymore.

Speak peace into the parts of her that still panic.
Speak healing into the places that still hurt.
And speak truth that silences every lie she believed in
the dark.

Remind her that healing doesn't mean forgetting.
That grief is not weakness. And that You're not asking her
to carry this alone anymore.

Thank You for being the kind of God who sits in the ashes
with us—who restores not just what we lost, but who we
are.
That what tried to break her could still be the soil where
something beautiful grows.

Right here. right now, let her feel it.

In Jesus' name,
Amen.

Part Three

Where Redemption Rises

This is the sacred turning.

The moment when what was meant to bury you becomes the ground God builds upon.

Where sorrow doesn't get the final say—redemption does.

Where your history, no matter how dark, becomes the backdrop for glory.

Here, we stop surviving and start breathing again.
Here, we stop rehearsing the pain and begin reclaiming the promise.

Because God doesn't just rescue you from the fire—He steps into it with you.
And when He brings you out, you don't come out the same.

You come out refined.
You come out restored.
You come out rising.

This is the part of the story where shame begins to unravel.

Where trauma loses its grip.

Where the chains fall—not because you're strong, but because **grace is stronger**.

You were never meant to live under the weight of what happened to you.

You were meant to rise.

This isn't the end of your story.

It's the rebirth. So lift your eyes, beloved—because this is where redemption rises.

And this time... you rise with it.

Chapter 7

Trading Ashes for Beauty

The Unexpected Road to Restoration

Some stories don't end the way we expect.
They pause, they fracture, they fade into silence—only to reappear when we've long stopped looking.

By the time this chapter of my life began, I was no stranger to brokenness.
I had walked through betrayal, abandonment, grief—and the kind of love that leaves bruises you can't always see.

I had remarried, and I had divorced—again.
This time, it was from a man whose alcoholism unraveled our home before it ever had the chance to be whole

I wasn't looking for anything or anyone. I was simply surviving.

And then—God used something as ordinary as the internet to reintroduce someone I thought was gone for good.

Him.
My second husband.
The one who had once broken my heart.
The one I never expected to hear from again.

We didn't fall back into anything; there was no rush of romance—just conversation: raw, honest, and unfiltered.

Talks about what went wrong in his second marriage—
and in ours.
The kind of truth-telling we should've done years earlier,
but something was different this time.

We weren't pointing fingers.
We were holding mirrors.

We owned what we had broken.
We admitted the ways we had failed.
We listened with soft hearts instead of hard defenses.

And somewhere in the middle of all that truth, healing
began to peek through.

It wasn't dramatic or loud.
It was quiet. Sacred.
Like God was cracking open a door we had long since
sealed shut—just wide enough for grace to slip through.

I didn't know where it would lead.
But I knew this: God was writing something I never
thought I'd see again.

And all we had to do was stop rewriting the past long
enough to let Him restore what only He could.

Grace doesn't always arrive with fanfare.
Sometimes, it slips through the smallest opening—into a heart just barely willing to hope again.

- What part of your heart have you kept closed because disappointment got there first?

- Where might God be whispering gently—inviting you to open that sealed-off place again?

- If healing began not with answers but with surrender... would you be willing to crack the door?

"A new heart also will I give you, and a new spirit will I put within you: and I will take away the stony heart out of your flesh, and I will give you a heart of flesh." — Ezekiel 36:26 (KJV)

Raising Our Children Together – A Different Kind of Healing

Restoration didn't come with a grand gesture. It came quietly—through small, consistent choices to stay when leaving would've been easier

We weren't the same people anymore.
Life had humbled us.
Grief had changed us.
And somewhere in the in-between, God had done something holy.

He had never fathered children of his own.
But mine—already worn from the weight of loss—became his only chance to be a dad.

And he didn't just step into the role.
He grew into it.

Not with spotlight moments or picture-perfect memories,
But in the shadows—In the uncelebrated, difficult days that tested love more than affirmed it.

He didn't show up for Friday night games or school concerts—because our kids didn't have those.

They were navigating identity, wrestling with grief, trying to grow up with pieces of their foundation missing

But he was there for what mattered.
He stayed through the slammed doors.
Through the silence.
Through the hard years when "you're not my real Dad"
felt like a badge he never wanted to wear.

And here's the truth—they didn't aim their pain at him.
They aimed it at me.

I was the safe target.
The one who took the blame for the chaos they couldn't
name.
The one who bore the weight of their unspoken grief.

But even then... he stayed.

He didn't take it personally.
He didn't give up.
He just kept showing up.

He stood in the gap with quiet strength, offering a steady
presence when everything else felt like it was falling
apart.

And over time, something shifted.

The kids who once kept him at a distance started to lean
in—to call, to confide, to trust.

Now, as adults, when their lives feel like they're
unraveling, he's one of the first they reach for.

Because love like that leaves a mark.
Not a loud, performative one.
But the kind that stays.

He never had children by blood. But through the trials, the tears, and the tired prayers, he became a father.

Not because it was easy.
But because he chose to stay when others walked away.

His consistency didn't just change our home—it revealed the kind of love that heals what trauma once shattered.

Well Reflection – When Love Looks Like Staying

Sometimes love doesn't roar. It simply remains.
It doesn't always feel soft.

Sometimes, it's rugged and worn—tired from showing up when it would've been easier to disappear.

But that kind of love? It's holy.

- Have you ever been loved with quiet, unwavering strength? How did it impact you?

- Where in your life is God calling you to love through presence—not perfection?

"Beareth all things, believeth all things, hopeth all things, endureth all things. Charity never faileth..." — 1 Corinthians 13:7–8 (KJV)

The Woman Who Got a Second Chance at Love

When I think of the Samaritan woman, I don't just see her shame.
I see the empty places where love kept failing her.
I see the echo of rejection behind each relationship that collapsed.
The weight of starting over—again and again—and the silent ache of expecting disappointment.

But then came **Jesus.**

Not with shame.
Not with reminders of everything she'd done wrong.
But with Living Water.

He didn't just speak truth.
He spoke value.
He didn't just point out the pattern.
He revealed her worth.

He offered her something no one else had—a chance to be fully known and still fully chosen.

That's what restoration looks like.
Not the filtered version of love people post online.
Not the polished version we pretend to have figured out.
But the sacred rebuilding of a heart that had been broken too many times.

That was us.

Two people bruised by the past.
Two stories scarred by betrayal, failure, and loss.
Two hearts that had stopped believing healing was even possible.

But Jesus met us at the well too.
He reminded me I wasn't too far gone to be loved well.
He reminded my husband that legacy isn't just biology—
It's presence, faithfulness, and the courage to start again.

We didn't get here because we figured it all out.
We got here because *He* never gave up on us.

Grace didn't just show up once.
It rebuilt us—one surrendered choice at a time.

And in that sacred space, He turned ashes into beauty.
Not in a moment.
But over time.
Step by step.
Yes after yes.

And the woman who once wondered if she'd ever be loved again—found herself living in the overflow of a love she never could have earned.

She was no longer the woman defined by brokenness.
She was the woman rewritten by grace.
One who dared to believe again.
And saw beauty rise from ashes.

"And I will restore to you the years that the locust hath eaten..." — Joel 2:25 (KJV)

Well Reflection – When Beauty Begins to Rise

Sometimes beauty doesn't burst through the ashes.
It grows slow—nurtured by forgiveness, watered by grace, and warmed by presence.

- What have you walked through that felt like ruin— but might actually be a resurrection in process?

- Where are you beginning to see beauty in places that once only held pain?

- Are you willing to believe that your most painful season could become the most fruitful?

"They that sow in tears shall reap in joy." — Psalm 126:5 (KJV)

Facing the Ache – When Love Comes With Scars

There's a sacred tension in choosing someone again—not because you've forgotten the pain.
Not because it wasn't real.
But because something deeper in you dares to hope.

Maybe the healing didn't come with a moment of clarity or a dramatic turning point.
Maybe it looked like holding your breath when the door opened again
And **whispering with shaky hope, "Please don't break me this time."**

This is the ache that comes with reconciliation.
The ache of trusting what once hurt you.
Of offering your heart again—even when it carries the memory of what it took to survive last time.

And here's what no one tells you:
It's not weakness to feel the scar after the wound has closed.
It's not failure to remember the pain even while walking in healing.
It's just the reminder that grace didn't erase the past—it redeemed it.

So let yourself feel it.

Not as proof that you're stuck...
But as evidence that something once shattered is being rebuilt.
That the ache is not your enemy—it's a sign you're still tender, still open, still reaching.

And in the middle of that ache, God is near.
He is not waiting for you to be fearless.
He's sitting in the ache with you—rebuilding what was broken...
Brick by brick, breath by breath, day by day.

 "And the Lord shall guide thee continually, and satisfy thy soul in drought... and thou shalt be like a watered garden."
— Isaiah 58:11 (KJV)

Pour It Out – When You're Afraid to Hope Again

This is your space.
Not to be perfect.
Not to tie it all up in a bow.
But to be real.

Maybe you've loved someone who let you down.

Maybe you've forgiven more than once and still felt the sting.

Maybe you're trying to rebuild a connection that still carries cracks—and you wonder if you're foolish for even trying.

You're not.
You're brave.

Maybe the people in your life don't understand why you said yes again.
Maybe you're still trying to figure that out, too.

But grace rarely follows logic.
And healing almost never travels in straight lines.

So pour it out here.

The doubts that creep in when no one's watching.
The memories that rise unexpectedly and try to shake your trust.

The prayers you whisper with guarded hope,
like "Lord, *please let this time be different.*"

Tell Him about the boundaries you had to rebuild.
The parts of your heart you're still afraid to uncover.
The ache that reminds you of how much it cost you last
time.

Ask the hard questions.
Speak the truth that still feels unfinished.
Then pause... and let God respond.

Not just with **reassurance**, but with **restoration.**

Let Him remind you that your tenderness is not a liability.

It's the soil where something sacred is growing.
That your story isn't weak because it's been through so
much—It's holy because *you're still here*.

"*Fear not; for thou shalt not be ashamed: neither be thou*
confounded; for thou shalt not be put to shame... for thy
Maker is thine husband; the Lord of hosts is His name." —
Isaiah 54:4–5 (KJV)

A Prayer for the One Who's Still Afraid to Trust Again

Lord,
You see her.
The one who's reading these words with guarded hope.
The **one who's dared to keep going, even after the pieces of her life fell apart more than once.**

The one who wants to believe that love can be safe again... but still hears the echoes of what broke her last time.

You know the battles she's fought that no one else saw.

The silent decisions she's made just to keep her heart from shattering again.

You see the strength it takes for her to hope—and the fear she hides behind every "I'm fine."

God, she's tired of surviving.
Tired of building walls.
Tired of pretending she doesn't still ache.

But she **doesn't know how to let the walls down**—not without wondering if she'll be left exposed again.
So meet her there, Lord.
In that fragile in-between space where fear and faith collide.

Speak gently to her scars.
Not with pressure, but with presence.

Let her know she doesn't have to rush her healing—but she doesn't have to do it alone either. Remind her that trust isn't about forgetting what happened.

It's about believing that You can make something beautiful in spite of it.
That You're not asking her to ignore the pain—but to hand it to You so You can begin the restoration.

Tell her again, Lord—that she's not foolish for loving, not weak for forgiving, not broken beyond repair.

Give her the kind of peace that calms the storm inside.
The kind of love that doesn't flinch at her story.
The kind of strength that lets her rest, not just resist.

And when she's tempted to pull away again to protect herself from what feels too risky—wrap her in the safety of Your arms.
Because You don't just stay.
You restore.

Hold her heart with tenderness, God.
She's not asking for perfection—just proof that she won't have to walk this next part alone.
And You, Jesus—You've never walked away.

Amen.

"Yea, I have loved thee with an everlasting love: therefore with lovingkindness have I drawn thee." — Jeremiah 31:3 (KJV)

So if you're standing at the edge of a second chance, unsure if you can trust again—may this chapter remind you: God restores differently than the world does

This isn't just the story of reconciliation—it's the story of how grace tenderly gathers every broken piece... and dares to begin again.

Chapter 8
The Power of Your Testimony

When Silence No Longer Serves You

After finding restoration, the next step wasn't silence—it was speaking.

Because healing isn't just about what God does in you.

It's about what He wants to do through you.

But here's the truth:

Silence won't heal what God is asking you to speak.

"And they overcame him by the blood of the Lamb, and by the word of their testimony..." – Revelation 12:11 (KJV)

Your story carries power.
Not just because you survived—but because your survival points to a Savior.
Not just because you made it—but because God brought you through.

And maybe your voice has been shaking.
Maybe you've questioned whether anyone would even care.
But someone needs to hear it.
Because when you speak... chains break.

When the Shame Starts to Break Off

For so long, shame convinced you to stay quiet.
It wrapped itself around your voice like chains,
whispering:

"People will judge you."
"They'll never understand."
"Your past is too messy."
"You should've known better."

And maybe you believed it.
Maybe you let silence become your safety.
But God never meant for you to carry that weight.

Shame doesn't lose its power in the dark.
It loses its power *in the light*.

And your testimony?
It's not about exposing your failures.
It's about exalting your freedom.

**You're not telling your story to glorify the pain—you're
telling it to glorify the God who *healed* you from it.**

*"For ye were sometimes darkness, but now are ye light in
the Lord: walk as children of light." – Ephesians 5:8 (KJV)*

You don't have to stay silent anymore.
Your story is no longer a source of shame—it's a seed God will use to grow something beautiful.

Well Reflection – When Silence Feels Safer than Honesty

- Have you ever kept quiet about your story out of fear of judgment or rejection?

- What parts of your testimony still carry a sense of shame—and what would it take to bring them into the light?

- How might your healing become someone else's hope if you dared to speak?

"Let the redeemed of the Lord say so, whom he hath redeemed from the hand of the enemy." – Psalm 107:2 (KJV)

When You Let Your Story Speak

There is something sacred about a story told in truth.

Not polished, not filtered, not wrapped in a bow to make it easier for others to digest—but real.

Because the truth is, the most powerful testimonies aren't the ones that make us look good.
They're the ones that make God look faithful.

When I first began to share my story—the real one—I didn't know what would happen.
I was afraid.

Afraid people would turn away.
Afraid they'd judge the past, I had worked so hard to survive.
Afraid they'd only see the broken parts and miss the beauty God was building.

But something unexpected happened.

People leaned in.

Not because I was strong, but because they saw their own pain in my honesty.
Not because I had all the answers, but because I wasn't pretending anymore.

And somehow...
That gave them permission to stop pretending too.

Your testimony isn't just about what you've been through.
It's about what *didn't* destroy you.
It's about the *One* who carried you through it.

And every time you tell the truth—about the pain, the healing, the God who met you in the middle of it all—you plant seeds in someone else's soul.

Seeds of hope.
Seeds of courage.
Seeds of healing.

Because testimony breaks chains—not just for you,
But for the one who's still waiting to believe healing is possible.

Well Reflection - When God Uses Your Voice to Set Others Free

- What part of your story do you feel most afraid to speak aloud?

- Who might need to hear the truth you've been carrying in silence?

- How could your scars become a map for someone else's healing?

I have not hid thy righteousness within my heart; I have declared thy faithfulness and thy salvation: I have not concealed thy lovingkindness and thy truth from the great congregation." — Psalm 40:10 (KJV)

From Shame to Strength Testimony Transforms Identity

For a long time, shame was the loudest voice in my story.

It told me I was disqualified.
It whispered that no one would understand.
It convinced me that silence was safer than truth.

So I stayed quiet.

I wore strength like armor—but underneath, I was still hiding.

Hiding from what people might say.
Hiding from the memories I hadn't made peace with.
Hiding from the version of myself I didn't want to revisit.

But here's what I've learned:

Shame loses its grip the moment you stop hiding.

It thrives in silence.
But it dies in the light.

And testimony?
Testimony is light.

The very stories the enemy tried to use to shame me—God now uses to set others free.

The broken pieces I once buried?
They became the very ground where healing took root.

The words I was too afraid to speak?
They became bridges for others to cross their own valleys of pain.

Because when you own your story, it stops owning you.
And when you let God redeem it, your identity is no longer
what happened to you—it's who He's forming within you.

You are not the sin.
You are not the mistake.
You are not the label someone else gave you.

You are the redeemed.
You are the healed.
You are the testimony walking.

And every time you speak, the chains that held you and
someone else begin to break.

- What parts of your story have you been hiding because of shame?

- What would it look like to let God use even those places for His glory?

- How might your identity shift if you believed your scars were proof of strength—not signs of failure?

"I shall not die, but live, and declare the works of the Lord."
– Psalm 118:17 (KJV)

Letting Your Story Break Chains – A Legacy of Boldness

There comes a point in the healing journey when silence stops feeling safe, and starts feeling like suffocation.

You've wept through nights no one knew about.

You've walked roads that tried to break you.

You've witnessed God breathe purpose into pain

But the world still only sees the surface.

They don't know the fire you walked through to get here.
They don't know the nights you prayed with no words left
to speak.
They don't know how close you came to giving up.

And maybe...
You haven't told them.

Maybe you've kept your story tucked away because it felt
safer that way.
Maybe you've convinced yourself that your voice didn't
matter.
That your pain was too personal.
That your scars were still too fresh.

But friend—your story was never meant to stay buried.

Because when God heals you, He doesn't just restore you
for you.
He restores you for them.
The ones still stuck in the place you thought you'd never
escape.

Testimony is what turns pain into purpose.
It's what takes what the enemy meant to silence you—and
turns it into a megaphone for God's grace.

You're not just a survivor.
You're a speaker of truth.
A chain-breaker.
A light bearer.

And every time you open your mouth to tell the truth of what God has done—heaven takes notice, hell trembles, and someone else dares to believe healing is possible for them, too.

Well Reflection – When God Uses the Story You Tried to Forget

- Who in your life might need to hear the parts of your story you've kept silent?

- What fears have held you back from sharing more openly?

- What if your breakthrough is someone else's lifeline?

"I will declare thy name unto my brethren: in the midst of the congregation will I praise thee." — Psalm 22:22 (KJV)

When God Uses Your Story – Even the Messy Parts

We all want a story that's easy to tell.
Clean lines, happy endings, nothing too vulnerable.
But those aren't the stories that heal people.

The ones that break chains?
They're the ones with raw edges.

With moments that make you pause before speaking
them out loud.
With chapters you thought you'd never be able to say
without crying.

*But God isn't waiting for your story to be pretty—He's
waiting for it to be real.*

**Because the moment you stop hiding what you've been
through, is the moment someone else stops believing
they're alone.**

Maybe you've spent years trying to forget parts of your
past.

**Maybe you've asked God to use you, but you didn't expect
Him to point back to the things you wanted to erase.**

But He will.
*Because nothing is wasted in the hands of the One who
redeems.*

Not the heartbreak.
Not the divorce.
Not the addiction, the abuse, the anxiety, the grief.
Not even the years you walked away from Him.

Every scar becomes a signpost.
Every tear becomes a testimony.
Every weakness becomes a stage for His power to shine through.

Your story isn't disqualified because it's messy—it's qualified because it reveals a Savior who didn't flinch at the mess.

So tell it.
Even if your voice shakes.
Even if not everyone claps.
Even if it's still tender when you speak it.

Because if it points to Jesus—it's worth telling.

Facing the Ache – When Your Story Still Stings to Tell

Have you ever felt the weight of your story pressing on your chest—not because you're ashamed of it, but because it still hurts to speak it out loud?

Maybe you've tried to bury it, minimize it, or convince yourself it doesn't matter anymore.

But it does.

Because someone out there is walking through what you barely survived—and your silence won't save them.
Your story will.

Maybe you're afraid that if you say it out loud, people will look at you differently.
Maybe you're scared they'll see your weakness.
But what if they see God's strength instead?

What if the very thing you've kept hidden…
Is the very thing God wants to use?

This ache you carry isn't proof you've failed—it's proof you've lived.
It's proof you've *overcome.*

So today, let yourself feel the sting.
Not to dwell there—but to hand it to the Healer who turns pain into power.

"Many, O Lord my God, are thy wonderful works which thou hast done… if I would declare and speak of them, they are more than can be numbered." – Psalm 40:5 (KJV)

Pour It Out – When Your Story Still Feels Fragile

This is your invitation to stop hiding the parts of your story that still feel unfinished.

The chapters you've kept tucked away because they're too complicated to explain.

The memories that surface when you least expect them—raw, real, and full of emotion.

What if those are the very places God wants to use?

What if the words you've never spoken could be the balm someone else has been waiting for?

Take a moment to pour it all out here.

Write from the place that still wrestles with shame.

The moment you thought, "No one would understand if they knew."

The fear that your story is too messy to be used.

The weight of the silence you've carried for years.

Then ask Jesus to meet you there.

Invite Him to sit with you in the pages of your pain.

To help you see your testimony not as a liability—but as a weapon against the very darkness that tried to silence you.

And as you write, don't hold back.

Let Him show you what He sees when He looks at your story.
Let Him speak worth over every scar.
Let Him remind you:

This isn't just your survival.
It's someone else's breakthrough.

"Come and hear, all ye that fear God, and I will declare what he hath done for my soul." — Psalm 66:16 (KJV)

A Prayer for the One Still Learning to Speak Their Story

Lord,
You see her—the one who's reading these words with
tears in her eyes and weight in her chest.
The one who's lived through more than she's ever told.
The one who's spent years surviving... but has stayed
silent.

She's carried shame like a secret.
She's carried strength like a shield.
She's convinced herself that her story was too messy to
matter.
Too complicated to share.
Too painful to relive.

But You, Lord—You were there in every chapter.
In the trauma that tried to steal her voice.
In the sorrow that shaped her.
In the moments she thought, "I'll never speak of this again."
And still... You called her chosen.

So today, I pray for the courage to speak. Not from a
place of *perfection*—but from a place of *freedom*.

Remind her that her testimony is not a liability.
It's a **light.**
A *weapon*.
A *seed that will bear fruit in someone else's healing*.

Silence may have protected her before, but now, God—
let her story speak.

Let it echo with hope.
Let it break chains she doesn't even see.
Let it be the evidence of what You've done.

Heal what still aches.
Strengthen what still trembles.
And make her brave in the telling.

Because her voice matters.
Because her story isn't over.
Because what the enemy meant for harm, You are
already using for good.

Let her speak, Lord.
Let her rise.
Let her believe that her healing and her testimony can live
in the same breath.

And let the fruit of her brokenness bring life to someone
else's dry ground.

In Jesus' name, Amen.

"Your testimony isn't just your past—it's your purpose.
And the world needs your voice."

Chapter 9

From the Well to the World

When the Call Finds You in the Mess

The woman at the well didn't walk away quietly.

She didn't stop to perfect her image or clean up her story before running back into town.

She left her jar behind—and with it, the shame that had defined her.

And she became something no one expected:

A voice.

A vessel.

A witness.

"The woman then left her waterpot, and went her way into the city, and saith to the men, Come, see a man..." — John 4:28–29 (KJV)

She didn't go to seminary.

She didn't wait to be qualified.

She just went.

And that's how calling usually works.

It doesn't show up when your life is tidy.

It finds you in the middle of the mess—when you're tired, stretched thin, and wondering if anything you've lived through could ever be used for something eternal.

That's where it found me, too.

When Nursing Became Ministry

I didn't just become a nurse.
I became a witness.
A witness to both agony and glory.
To hell and healing.

To the places where life begins... and the moments when
it ends.

God didn't lead me into sanitized spaces—He led me into
the rooms where grief howled, where families shattered,
and where mothers said goodbye far too soon.

I stood beside incubators that hummed with hope and
fear.
Held hands with parents who were drowning in sorrow.
Prayed silently over babies born addicted, born dying,
born into chaos.
I cared for veterans with stories that broke my heart.
Men and women who still fought battles in their minds
long after the war ended.

I wasn't just changing dressings and charting vitals.
I was standing in the space between heartbreak and
heaven—and asking God to meet us there.

"Bear ye one another's burdens, and so fulfil the law of
Christ." — Galatians 6:2 (KJV)

It was sacred work.
Not because it was glamorous.
But because it was holy.

There were days I went home and cried in the shower.
There were nights I stayed up praying for the family I had just walked through death with.

There were moments when I wondered if my heart could take another ounce of pain.

But I stayed.
Because God stayed with me.

He had walked me through hospital corridors as a mother.
Now, He walked with me into those same spaces as a nurse.

And somehow, the pain I had lived through became the place He used to heal others.

- Have you ever questioned if the pain you've lived through has a purpose?

- What sacred spaces has God trusted you to walk into—not despite your story, but because of it?

- How might your personal healing equip you to walk others through theirs?

"But we have this treasure in earthen vessels, that the excellency of the power may be of God, and not of us." – 2 Corinthians 4:7 (KJV)

From the NICU to the Nations – A Calling Born Through Crisis

I didn't always see myself as someone called...

All of my children were born prematurely—but it was my youngest daughter, a micro-preemie born fifteen weeks early, who marked me the most.

My tiniest warrior.
She entered the world with a silence that shook me.
Too delicate to cry. Too raw for the world.

But even in that silence, she carried something eternal.
I didn't just watch her fight—I watched heaven lean close.
In those long months beside her, I saw God's hand rest on both of us.

I didn't just pray—I surrendered.
 I didn't just ask God to heal her—I asked Him to use me.

And somewhere between those sacred midnight hours and the weary sunrises that followed, a deeper calling was born.

Not just to be a nurse—but to be a vessel.
Not just to survive—but to say yes to something holy that was forming through the ache.

God was showing me: this wasn't just about saving one life.
It was about letting Him reshape mine.

I walked those corridors with a kind of faith I didn't even know I had—whispering life over a baby wrapped in wires, singing praise songs over a plastic incubator, asking God to trade my breath for hers if it came to that.

And somewhere in the middle of all of that pain... purpose was born.
I didn't just become a nurse to earn a living.
I became a nurse because healing had walked through my own house.

"He healeth the broken in heart, and bindeth up their wounds." – Psalm 147:3 (KJV)

I had carried a child too small for this world—and watched God sustain her.
I had cried prayers through sleepless nights—and watched God answer.

I had sat with pain—and learned how to stay.
So when I held a patient's hand, I brought more than medical skill.

I brought the sacred ache of a mother who had already met suffering face-to-face... and still chose to believe.

I brought compassion that came from the trenches, not textbooks.

And when I cared for other tiny ones fighting for a chance at life, for grieving families, or for veterans haunted by memories they could not escape—I understood the weight they carried.

Because I had carried it too.

That's the thing about purpose.

It rarely starts on a stage.

It usually starts in a storm.

Well Reflection – When Purpose Finds You in the Storm

- What sacred places has God walked you through that might become part of your calling?

- How has your personal suffering prepared you to serve others with deeper compassion?

- What if the places you prayed hardest in are the very places He's now sending you back into—with healing in your hands?

"Comfort ye, comfort ye my people, saith your God." – Isaiah 40:1 (KJV)

When Healing Becomes the Assignment

Some callings don't come wrapped in clarity.
They come wrapped in ache.

Mine looked like hospital cribs and tear-streaked cheeks.
Like mothers too numb to cry, and fathers too broken to
speak.

I cared for babies born into suffering—fragile bodies
trembling from the ache of withdrawal they never chose.

And when I held them close, I didn't see shame.

I saw their story.

Because I had once loved someone who was devoured by
addiction's grip.

But now, I wasn't drowning in the wreckage.

I was steady in the storm.

**And in that sacred reversal, I felt mercy not as a word—but
as a calling.**

I saw it in the eyes of mothers who wanted to break the
cycle, but didn't know how.

They weren't monsters.
*They were women marked by trauma—still trying to believe
they were worthy of freedom.*

And then there were the children with conditions no one could fix.
Genetic diagnoses that stole breath, futures, and milestones before they even had a chance to be reached.

I sat with parents who knew the calendar was not on their side.
There would be no first steps, no kindergarten backpacks, no teenage eye-rolls.
Just a fragile heartbeat, a short-lived giggle, and the holy ache of loving a child you know you'll one day bury.

There was no roadmap for that kind of ministry.
Only presence.
Only compassion.
Only the kind of sacred stillness that says, I see you. I'm not going anywhere.

And in those moments, I knew this wasn't just a career—it was an assignment.

I wasn't there to fix what was broken.
I was there to carry the weight.
To sit in the ashes and still believe beauty was possible.

Because healing doesn't always mean curing.
Sometimes, it means holding someone's hand while they break...
And refusing to let go.

"Blessed are the merciful: for they shall obtain mercy." —
Matthew 5:7 (KJV)

Well Reflection – When You Carry What Can't Be Cured

- Have you ever been the one called to stay when others stepped back?

- To help someone plan for goodbye—while your own heart quietly shattered beside them?

- What did those moments teach you about the sacredness of presence?

- Where might God be asking you now to stand in the gap for someone who cannot carry their sorrow alone?

"To every thing there is a season, and a time to every purpose under the heaven: A time to weep, and a time to laugh; a time to mourn, and a time to dance." —
Ecclesiastes 3:1,4 (KJV)

I had spent years walking through rooms where healing
didn't always mean miracles—but presence.
And somewhere in the sacred stillness of holding space
for others, God began stirring something in me, too.

A gentle but undeniable shift.
A quiet ache that said,

"This season is closing... but I'm not done writing your story."

I didn't know what it would look like.
I only knew He was inviting me to follow—not just into
hospital rooms, but into the wide open.

Into purpose that moved.
Into healing that journeyed.

Into the kind of calling that doesn't just stay still—it sets you in motion.

When Faith Hits the Road – Living on Purpose Wherever He Sends You

By the time the kids were grown, something in our lives
began to shift.
It wasn't loud or dramatic—just a holy stirring.
An ache that said, "There's more."
Not more success. Not more security.
More surrender.
More purpose.

We packed up our lives into an RV and hit the road.
Not to escape—but to follow.
To follow the call of a God who doesn't just send you into
hospitals and homes, He sends you into the wide open.
Into the breathtaking, the unexpected, the wild places
where His glory can't be denied.

And we saw it.
Oh, we saw it.

We stood on the rim of the Grand Canyon...A place so
surreal, it felt like walking inside a movie set.

**The colors, the silence, the immensity—it left us speechless.
Because only God could carve something that sacred out
of dust.**

We traced the rugged cliffs of the Oregon coast—Waves crashing with wild praise, fog curling over pine-lined cliffs, sea spray clinging to our cheeks like a blessing.
It didn't feel like sightseeing.
It felt like worship.

We journeyed up the coast of Maine and back down through the Carolinas to Florida.

Then west again into stories, friendships, and moments that could only have been written by the Author of it all.

We made friends in Louisiana who taught us the real meaning of "going Cajun" where joy was served as generously as Fresh seafood, and friends became extended family that lived in another state.

In Colorado, we stood in reverent awe at a pow wow held at Garden of the Gods.

We watched Native American warriors pray over our military soldiers—calling on the name of Jesus with voices that trembled with power.

It felt like heaven touching earth.
Like wounds meeting worship.
Like the kind of unity only the Spirit of God can knit together.

And through it all, my husband—who had once watched me live this life of nursing and calling—joined the mission in his own way.

He became a travel nurse recruiter, working remotely so we could journey together.
He wasn't just sending nurses across the country
He was sending us.

Every stop was more than a pin on a map.
It was a divine appointment.
A place where God's beauty met our brokenness, and we found healing in the wide-open spaces.

Because when you say yes to God's purpose...
He doesn't just use your gifts.
He uses your whole story.
Your marriage. Your journey. Your surrender.

He sends you not just with assignments—but with anointing.

And every mile we traveled, every person we met, every awe-struck moment of creation we witnessed, it all whispered the same thing:

"This is what purpose looks like—when your life becomes the well."

- Where has God already been revealing His glory in the ordinary rhythms of your life?

- What places or people have left you breathless with awe—and how might they be part of your assignment?

- Have you considered that your story, your surrender, and even your travels could become someone else's well?

"For the earth shall be filled with the knowledge of the glory of the Lord, as the waters cover the sea." — Habakkuk 2:14 (KJV)

Facing the Ache – When Purpose Feels Bigger Than You

There comes a moment in every journey with God where the weight of calling feels heavier than expected.

Not because you're unwilling—but because you wonder if you're enough.

You've lived through so much.
You've poured out your heart in hidden places.
You've stayed when others would've walked away.

But still...
Something inside questions if you're really the one.

Maybe you've told yourself:
"I'm too broken."
"My story is too messy."
"I missed my chance."

But what if the ache you're feeling isn't disqualification?
What if it's sacred confirmation?

The ache of knowing the call is bigger than you—because it's supposed to be.
The ache of sensing that you're being stretched—not to break, but to overflow.

Pause here.
Take a breath.
Let the ache speak honestly.

And then let God speak louder.

Pour It Out – When Your Story Becomes the Well

You didn't ask for the fire you walked through.
You didn't plan the detours, the heartbreak, the ache that became your teacher.
But here you are—still standing, still breathing, still called.

And now... God is asking for your story.

Not the polished version.
Not the one with the pain edited out.
The real one. The poured-out one.
The one that bleeds mercy and whispers, "I've been there too."

Because your scars don't disqualify you.
They anoint you.

What part of your story once felt too broken to be used— but now glimmers with redemption?

Where has God asked you to carry others—not in strength, but in sacred surrender?

Have you seen moments in your life that felt ordinary— but now you realize were holy?

Write them out. Then speak truth back over every one.

Where is God asking you to pour right now?

Into a person, a place, a calling ? Be bold, be specific.

"And if any man thirst, let him come unto me, and drink. He that believeth on me... out of his belly shall flow rivers of living water." – John 7:37–38 (KJV)

Let this entry be your altar.
Let these pages hold your yes.

You are not just carrying a testimony—you are becoming the well.

A Prayer for You Poured Out with Purpose

Beloved,
You've made it through storms that could've drowned you.
You've carried jars of shame, survival, and sacrifice longer than most people will ever know.
But this, right here, is holy ground.

This is where purpose takes root.

This is where God says:
"You are no longer just the one who carries pain—you are the one who carries My power."

So as you breathe in these final words of the chapter, don't just read them—*receive them.*

Let's pray

Jesus,
You see them.
Not as someone barely getting by—but as someone You have anointed to walk with healing in their hands.
They've carried pain in silence.

They've loved through rejection, prayed through heartbreak, and served in places the world never applauded.
But Heaven saw every tear.
Every "yes" when it hurt.
Every moment they stayed when they wanted to run.

And now, God, You are stirring something deeper.
You are awakening the truth.

This life is not wasted. This story is not disqualified.
This heart still beats with purpose.

So, right now—send them.
Not when they feel ready.
Not when their life is polished.
Send them now—right in the rawness of their
obedience.

Let their words speak life.
Let their wounds release compassion.
Let their story water dry places and remind the world that
healing is real—and You are near.

Break off every lie that says they're too late, too broken,
or too ordinary.
Anoint them for such a time as this.
May their journey become *worship.*
May their surrender become *strength.*
May their *whole life become a well—***overflowing with**
Your Living Water.
And when they step out from this page,
Let them carry not just courage—but commissioning.

In Jesus' powerful name,
Amen

Therefore with joy shall ye draw water out of the wells of salvation. And in that day shall ye say, Praise the Lord, call upon his name, declare his doings among the people, make mention that his name is exalted."— Isaiah 12:3–4 (KJV)

Chapter 10

The Untold Story of the First Evangelist

Her story didn't end at the well. It was only the beginning

The story we often hear about, the woman at the well, centers on one unforgettable afternoon.
A dusty road.
A heavy jar.
A shame-worn woman just trying to make it through the day.

And then—Jesus.

A life-changing conversation that shattered the silence, pierced the shame, and awakened something inside her she didn't know was still alive.

But what if that moment was never meant to stand alone?

What if the encounter at the well wasn't the end of her story—but the beginning?

She didn't just leave a jar behind that day.
She walked away from the silence.
She walked away from the labels.
She walked away from the life that once defined her
And she didn't fade into the background once the encounter ended.

She *ran.*
Back into the very village that had rejected her.
Not to hide.
But to *tell*, to testify, and to declare.
To invite others into the freedom she had just found.

"Come, see a man, which told me all things that ever I did: is not this the Christ?" – John 4:29 (KJV)

That moment wasn't just personal—it was powerful.
It wasn't just healing—it was a *commissioning.*

And according to early Christian tradition, her story didn't stop there.

She boldly preached the gospel throughout the Roman Empire.
She stood before Emperor Nero himself and declared Jesus as King.
And when threatened with torture, she didn't cower—*she rejoiced.*

She was no longer the woman at the well.
She had become a woman of the Word.

Because when Jesus redeems a life, He never stops at healing. He sends, He commissions, He multiplies what once felt disqualified and turns it into a message the world can't ignore.

And the same Jesus who met her that day is still calling us to do the same.

He's still turning silence into stories.
He's still turning shame into strength.
He's still turning broken women into bold witnesses.

And now the invitation is yours.
Will you stay at the well—or will you step into the story
He's still writing through you?

*"Ye have not chosen me, but I have chosen you, and
ordained you, that ye should go and bring forth fruit..."* —
John 15:16 (KJV)

Well Reflection – When Your Jar No Longer Fits the Journey

Sometimes what you've been carrying can't go with you into what God is calling you into.

The jar that once served a purpose has been left behind— you're not the same woman anymore.

- What are you still holding that no longer serves the woman God is raising up in you?

- What would it look like to lay it down—not out of shame, but out of trust?

- Is it possible the thing you're afraid to let go of is the very thing Jesus is asking you to leave behind?

"Cast thy burden upon the Lord, and he shall sustain thee..." — Psalm 55:22 (KJV)

Her True Name is Photini – From Outcast to Enlightened One

Most of us know her only by the parts of her story people whispered about.
She's remembered by her shame, not her strength.
By her past, not her purpose.

But that's not where her story ends.

Early Christian tradition tells us her name, *Photini*, meaning *"the enlightened one."*
It's more than a name.
It's a declaration of what Jesus did in her life.

"The entrance of thy words giveth light; it giveth understanding unto the simple." — Psalm 119:130 (KJV)

She didn't just meet the Messiah at the well—she met the truth about who she really was.

A woman once bound by silence... became a voice that couldn't be silenced.

A woman who once lived in the shadows... became a witness who radiated light.

A woman known by the eyes that looked down on her... became a woman chosen and commissioned by the One who looked into her.

Her name—Photini—tells the world:
Jesus didn't leave her the way He found her.
He turned her pain into purpose.
He turned her story into a legacy.
And He does the same for us.
Maybe you've felt nameless.
Maybe you've been known only by your struggles.
Maybe you've been remembered more for your mess than
for your meaning.
But in Christ, the story shifts.

"They looked unto him, and were lightened: and their faces were not ashamed." — Psalm 34:5 (KJV)

You don't have to be defined by what happened.
You don't have to be remembered for what broke you.
You can be called something new—because the One who
calls you knows you, and He calls you His.

"I have called thee by thy name; thou art mine." — Isaiah
43:1 (KJV)

- What false identity have you carried so long, it began to feel like truth?

- What would it mean to believe—deep down—that you are known not by your failures, but by His favor?

- Can you hear Him calling you by a name that's never been spoken over you before? What is it?

"And in that day shall the Lord of hosts be for a crown of glory, and for a diadem of beauty... to them that are turned to righteousness." — Isaiah 28:5 (KJV)

Sent with a Story – The Mission of Photini

Photini didn't fade into the background after meeting Jesus at the well.

She was never meant to be a footnote in someone else's gospel story.

She was a forerunner—a missionary, a martyr, a messenger of the Messiah.

Early church history tells us that her encounter with Christ launched her into bold ministry.
She didn't just share her story with her village—she carried it across nations.

"For I am not ashamed of the gospel of Christ: for it is the power of God unto salvation..." – Romans 1:16 (KJV)

According to both Eastern Orthodox tradition and Western Christian writings, Photini traveled to North Africa, Carthage, and even Rome.
She preached the gospel publicly.
She baptized new believers.
She brought the Living Water she received to people who had never tasted grace.

And her courage came at a cost.

During the reign of Emperor Nero—a time marked by intense persecution of Christians—
Photini and her family were arrested.
She was brought before Nero himself.

But even in the face of death—she didn't flinch.
She stood like a woman who had already met the true King.
Because she had.

She is remembered not just as a woman with a past—but as a woman who stood unwavering for Christ...

Well Reflection – When Obedience Feels Like Risking Everything

Sometimes your yes to God won't make sense to anyone else—except the people your story is meant to reach.

- Where is God asking you to speak when it would feel safer to stay silent?

- What fears are trying to convince you that you're not ready yet?

- Could your obedience unlock someone else's freedom?

"Them that honour me I will honour..." — 1 Samuel 2:30 (KJV)

Even when it meant torture.
Even when it meant martyrdom.
Her story didn't end in that prison cell.
Her legacy lived on.

She is honored in the Eastern Orthodox Church as *Saint Photini, Equal to the Apostles.*

Her boldness became a beacon for early believers.
Her testimony outlived the emperor who tried to silence it.

She wasn't just a woman who met Jesus—she was a woman who carried Him to the world.

"How beautiful are the feet of them that preach the gospel of peace, and bring glad tidings of good things!" – Romans 10:15 (KJV)

When Your Story Becomes a Commission

What if your most painful chapter was heaven's favorite opening line?

Who could be waiting on the other side of your obedience?

Legacy isn't built in comfort—it's born in courage.

"Ye have not chosen me, but I have chosen you, and ordained you..." – John 15:16 (KJV)

Confronting Nero – A Fearless Witness

Photini's encounter with Jesus changed everything—but her journey didn't end at the well.

According to early church tradition, she became more than a woman with a testimony.
She became a fearless evangelist—a leader in the early church who boldly preached the gospel, even when it cost her everything.

Years after her transformation, Photini traveled to Carthage, proclaiming Christ with boldness and authority. Her message reached Roman authorities—and eventually, Emperor Nero himself.

When she was brought before him, Nero tried to intimidate her. He threatened torture, imprisonment, and death.

But Photini didn't flinch.

"I will speak of thy testimonies also before kings, and will not be ashamed." — Psalm 119:46 (KJV)

She looked Nero in the eyes and declared she had already met the true King—and His name was Jesus.

The same woman who once avoided her neighbors.. *now stood before the most feared man in the empire.*

The same woman who once carried shame.. *now carried the gospel into the heart of Roman power.*

The same woman who once drew water in silence.. *now poured out Living Water without fear.*

Nero had her tortured, beaten, and imprisoned.

Still—*she worshiped.*
Still—*she testified.*
Still—*she encouraged others who suffered beside her.*

And she wasn't alone.
Her five sisters and two sons, also believers, stood before Nero. They too refused to recant.

"We are troubled on every side, yet not distressed; we are perplexed, but not in despair; persecuted, but not forsaken; cast down, but not destroyed." – 2 Corinthians 4:8–9 (KJV)

Photini's faith was not fragile.
It was forged in fire, rooted in grace, and fearless unto death.

Eventually, Nero had her thrown down a dry well.

But the irony couldn't be missed—he threw a woman into a well, not realizing...
she had become one.

She didn't die forgotten.
She didn't die defeated.
She died as a living well—faithful to the end.

When Boldness Becomes Your Legacy

What part of your story is still waiting for you to speak with fearless faith?

Where is God asking you to step up—not later, but now—and be a voice for Him?

If future generations remembered your name, what would you want them to say about your courage?

"Be strong and of a good courage; be not afraid, neither be thou dismayed: for the Lord thy God is with thee whithersoever thou goest." — Joshua 1:9 (KJV)

The Well Still Speaks – Your Legacy Starts Here

You've followed the footsteps of a woman once known only by her shame...
And discovered she wasn't just redeemed—she was *commissioned.*

You've heard the echo of her jar hitting the ground—and maybe, in your own way, you've dropped yours too.
The weight you carried.
The labels you believed.
The story you thought was too messy to matter.

But now—here you are.
Still standing.
Still reading.
Still reaching for the Living Water that never runs dry.
And this moment?

It's not an ending.
It's a beginning.

Because God didn't carry you through the heartbreak, the healing, and the journey beyond the well just to leave you here.

He's calling you forward.

Like Photini.
Like me.
Like every woman who dares to believe her story still matters.

This is where survival becomes surrender.
Where scars become seeds.
Where your life becomes the well.

You are no longer the woman who was just trying to get through the day.
You are the one He's sending—to your family.
To your community.
To a world still dying of thirst.

So walk boldly.
Love deeply.
Speak freely.

And never forget:
The well wasn't the end of her story.
It wasn't the end of mine.
And it's not the end of yours. It's just the beginning.

The Final Pouring – When Her Story Becomes Yours

You've followed the journey—from rejection to restoration.
From shattered wells to sacred surrender.
You've seen my story unfold across hospital rooms and highways, across broken homes and mended hearts.

But this moment... this is no longer just my story.

It's yours.

You are the woman at the well.
Not because your shame defines you—but because your Savior met you there.

You've carried jars of survival.
You've poured into others until you felt empty.
You've waited by dry places, hoping someone would see the ache behind your strength.
And maybe, like her... you thought that would be the end of the story.

But here's the truth: **You were never meant to stay by the well. You were always meant to rise from it.**

She left her jar behind—and you can too.
She stepped into purpose—and so can you.
She faced kings with courage—and you will face your calling the same way: not in fear, but in *faith*.

This is your commission.
Not someday.
Not when you're more healed, more ready, or more "qualified."

Now

Because you are no longer just the one who met Jesus at the well.
You are the one who was *sent* from it.

And everything you've walked through—the trauma, the tears, the prayers no one heard but God—they've made you not just a survivor...

They've made you a well.

So go tell your story.
Live your testimony.
Become the voice someone else has been waiting for.
Let living water flow from the places that once held pain.

Let it be said of you: She drank deeply... and poured freely.

"Therefore with joy shall ye draw water out of the wells of salvation." — Isaiah 12:3 (KJV)

You didn't just survive—you became someone others draw strength from.
The same places where you once begged for healing—now pour out hope to others.

- What have you walked through that God is now using to nourish others?

- When did you realize your story wasn't just a rescue—but a release for someone else?

- What would it look like to fully embrace the truth that you are the well now?

"Out of his belly shall flow rivers of living water." — John 7:38 (KJV)

Facing the Ache – When You Realize You've Become the Well

There's a moment—after all the healing, all the breaking, all the rebuilding—when you stop looking for the well... and realize you've become one.

Not because the journey was easy.
Not because everything makes sense.
But because something sacred has taken root in you—and now, others drink from the story you carry.

Maybe you didn't ask for this kind of legacy.
Maybe you were just trying to survive the pain.
But God was writing something deeper.
Not just for you... but through you.

You are no longer defined by what broke you.
You are defined by the One who met you there.

And now, when others come thirsty—they find living water flowing through your words, your healing, your scars.

Pause here.
Let the weight of that settle.
What you once ached for—you now offer to others.

And the Lord shall guide thee continually, and satisfy thy soul in drought... and thou shalt be like a watered garden, and like a spring of water, whose waters fail not." — Isaiah 58:11 (KJV)

Pour It Out – When the Well Lives in You

You didn't walk through fire just to come out smelling like smoke.

You walked through it so that when others step into the heat, you'll know how to stand with them—without flinching.

You've cried the tears.
You've prayed the prayers.
You've waited by dry places, wondering if they'd ever overflow again.

And now... something has shifted.

You're no longer just the woman who met Jesus at the well.
You've become a well.
A vessel.
A voice.

In what moments have others come to you not for advice—but to be nourished by your presence?

How is God using your scars as sacred evidence that healing is possible?

If the world only knew you by your faith today—not your past—how would they describe you?

Where have you seen God transform your greatest wound into someone else's breakthrough?

"And if any man thirst, let him come unto me, and drink. He that believeth on me... out of his belly shall flow rivers of living water." — John 7:37–38 (KJV)

Let this entry be your altar.
Let these pages hold your commissioning.

You are not just a story being told—you are the well He is still pouring through.

A Prayer for the One Who Has Become the Well

Jesus,
She didn't just read this book—she *walked through it*.
She traced her own pain across these pages, stopped at
every scar, breathed deep in every moment that once
made her feel unworthy—and kept going.

She saw herself in the Samaritan woman—and now, she
sees herself in the sent one.

She's no longer the one waiting to be filled.
She's the one You're pouring through.

So Father—Bless her.

Bless the voice that now carries redemption.
Bless the scars that now shine with glory.
Bless the places in her story that once felt wasted—
because You're now using them to water the world.

Give her strength when the journey feels heavy.
Give her courage when the old lies whisper again.
Give her clarity to know when to speak...
And the grace to know when to just *be*.

Let her remember:

She carries the well within her now.

She is the miracle.
She is the evidence that grace still flows
And that Jesus still meets women by the water.

Let her story never run dry.
Let her legacy ripple through generations.
And let every word she speaks echo this truth:

"I have been with Jesus—and I will never be the same."

In Your name, Jesus,
Amen

"Go ye into all the world, and preach the gospel to every creature." — *Mark* 16:15 (KJV)

From My Heart to Yours

Dear Reader,

If you made it here, I want you to know—this isn't just a book.
It's a piece of my heart.

Every chapter you've read came from places I once tried to hide.
Places of shame.
Places of pain.
Places I thought God couldn't possibly use.

But He met me at my own well—more than once.
He saw every part of my story... and still called me worthy of redemption.

I was the woman with the past.
The woman carrying too much.
The woman who had lost more than she thought she could bear.

And yet—Jesus still came for me.

He didn't wait for me to clean it all up.
He sat beside me in the mess.
He offered Living Water when all I had was a jar full of survival.

And little by little, I began to leave it behind.

As I wrote this, I kept thinking of you.
The one who's been carrying a jar for far too long.

The one who's wondered if it's too late.
The one who loves Jesus but still wrestles with shame.

You are seen.
You are known.
You are loved.

This isn't the end of your story—it's the beginning of a new chapter.

Leave the jar.

Walk in freedom.
Speak your story.

Live like Photini—overflowing with grace, with purpose, with the kind of hope that sets others free.

I pray you never forget what He speaks to your heart in these pages:

You are not disqualified.
You are not too broken.
You are not behind.

You are chosen.
You are redeemed.
You are a living well.
You are deeply, relentlessly loved.

This wasn't just a book.
It was an invitation—

To leave behind the jar and become a living well.
To run—not away from your story, but into your calling.
To speak—not from perfection, but from redemption.

And if you ever need a reminder...
Come back to these pages.
Come back to the well.
Jesus will meet you here—again and again.

> "Being confident of this very thing,
> that he which hath begun a good work in you
> will perform it until the day of Jesus Christ."
> — Philippians 1:6 (KJV)

Whether you read this book alone
or with a circle of women chasing freedom together—
thank you.

Thank you for showing up.
For being honest.
For letting the story speak to the deep places in you.

Let's keep going.
Let's keep sharing.
Let's keep drawing others to the well.

With all my heart,
Pamela Bowen

I'd love to hear from you. Whether you're reaching out about speaking engagements, book inquiries, collaborations, or just want to share how *My Journey Beyond the Well* impacted you—your message matters.

Find Pamela at:

Email: pamelabowenauthor@gmail.com
Facebook: facebook.com/PamelaBowenBooks
Instagram: instagram.com/pamelabowenauthor/#
YouTube: youtube.com/@PamelaBowenAuthor
On the Web: pamelabowenauthor.com

Thank You for Reading

If *Beyond the Well* touched your heart, encouraged your faith, or spoke to you in a meaningful way, I'd be deeply honored if you would share it with someone who might need it too. Every shared story has the power to reach another well and offer hope.

You can also follow my journey and stay connected through my **Amazon Author Page**:

☞ amazon.com/stores/Pamela-Bowen

And if you feel led to leave a review, your feedback means the world. Reader reviews help others discover this message of redemption and grace.

☞ Leave a review on Amazon

From the bottom of my heart—thank you. Your time, your support, and your voice make a difference. I'm truly grateful.

With love and grace,
Pamela Bowen

www.ingramcontent.com/pod-product-compliance
Lightning Source LLC
Chambersburg PA
CBHW021623120626
46545CB00001B/366